FOOD AND DRINK

BOOK 4

D0280021

THE Food & Drink BOOK 4

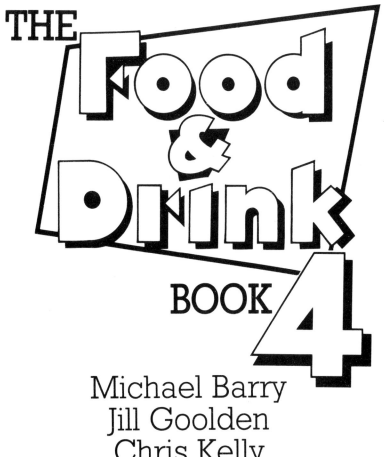

Michael Barry
Jill Goolden
Chris Kelly

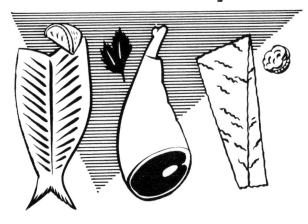

BBC BOOKS

Illustrations: Colin Hadley
Photographs: Sarah Taylor
Stylist: Rosein Neald
Home Economist: Mary Cadogan

The BBC would like to thank
Rosenthal Studio Haus Cutlery Limited
for the loan of the fork on page 66
and the spoon on page 88.

Published by BBC Books
A division of BBC Enterprises Limited
Woodlands, 80 Wood Lane
London W12 0TT

First published 1988
© Michael Barry, Jill Goolden, Chris Kelly 1988

ISBN 0 563 207086

Colour printing by Chorley and Pickersgill, Leeds
Photosetting by Ace Filmsetting Ltd, Frome, Somerset
Text and cover printed in Great Britain by
Richard Clay Ltd, Bungay, Suffolk

ACKNOWLEDGEMENTS

Food and Drink would like to thank the following for their help in the preparation of this book:

Judy Aitken
Jim Barnard
Carolyn Cavele
Fanny Craddock
Mike Dobson
Margaret Drake
Val Evans
Rev. John Fernley
David Gay
Henrietta Green
David Harrison
Pat Hennessy
John Inglis
Sabira Jaffer

Vicki Lawson-Brown
Frank Lincoln
Margaret Loh
Dr John Moillet
Roger Opie
Hans Schweitzer
Richard Shepherd
Marjorie Smedley
George and Amanda Streatfeild
Mick and Peg Sykes
Harold Tarrant
William Watters
Geoff and Mickie Wells
John Williams

CONTENTS

INTRODUCTION

Let's start with a few statistics: in the past four years *Food and Drink*'s Michael Barry has demonstrated 250 recipes to 375 million people. Jill Goolden has tasted (and spat out, she claims) 1,200 bottles of wine, to recommend 100 good buys. And Chris Kelly has presented more than 100 stories about the food industry (and had breakfast cooked for him in the studio by Michael Barry 75 times). In the same period the Barry/Goolden/Kelly team has sent out 400,000 fact sheets and sold 170,000 books.

Statistics, as we know from Disraeli and contemporary politics, are of dubious value. But the statistics above demonstrate two things – that *Food and Drink* is Britain's most popular television food programme, and that Chris Kelly has a healthy early-morning appetite. I will leave it to scholars with intellects more powerful than mine to ascertain which of these deductions is the more significant.

This is the *Food and Drink* team's fourth book. As with their previous confections, it is a stimulating blend of recipes from the series, down-to-earth drinking advice and a wide range of general food tips and news.

Not long ago I attended a dinner given by eight captains of the food industry. When I arrived in the oak-panelled dining room I discovered that I was on my own, facing the chairmen and managing directors of most of our major food companies. Here were the men who freeze, dehydrate and can the basic elements of our national diet and I was to sing for my supper. Their basic contention, albeit expressed in a civilised manner, was that the *Food and Drink* programme is biased against the food industry. I immediately agreed, partly because they were paying for dinner and it would have been churlish to contradict my hosts, and partly because in one sense we *are* biased. The fundamental purpose of the series is to encourage people to cook more of their own meals, using fresh ingredients (i.e. process their *own* food). If we succeed, they will obviously be buying less commercially processed food.

The word 'processed', however, is open to misinterpretation. There is nothing wrong with processed food *per se* – our wonderful, mature farmhouse cheddar is *processed*, and it is a *convenience* food, too, since cheese is a way of preserving milk.

Processed foods have played an important part in feeding an urban population since the Industrial Revolution. And convenience foods are crucial to families in which, perhaps, both parents work, and meals need to hit the table before the children begin to hit each other. But what is sad is that two whole generations have grown up with their palates dulled by an uninterrupted diet of low-grade processed foods – a nightmare world where 'tomato' sauce doesn't actually taste of tomato, where ice-cream doesn't have cream in it, where instant coffee bears no relation to the flavour of a roasted coffee bean. It is a 'Brave New World' in which the food technologist emerges from his laboratory like Baron Frankenstein, crying 'We have the technology . . . it is possible!' rather than being concerned whether its taste resembles that of the supposed raw materials, or whether it is in any way nutritious.

A grim and unrealistic vision? Not entirely. Up to the late seventies you could be forgiven for thinking the food technologist was king of a people without a sense or memory of taste. But the last decade has seen an explosion of consumer pressure, retail innovation and finally (and often reluctantly) a massive upgrading of quality and choice by food manufacturers.

In this context, the changes that product labelling have gone through in 20 years are very instructive. Here is the list of ingredients from a 1968 packet of Birds' (that is, General Foods') Angel Delight, butterscotch flavour:

INGREDIENTS: Sugar, Hydrogenated Vegetable Oil, Precooked Starch, Sodium Caseinate, Propylene Glycol Monopalmitate, Sodium Phosphate, Salt, Artificial Flavourings, Lecithin, and Artificial Colourings.

That list was the only consumer information on the packet, except for the home chemistry necessary to turn the above formula into a pudding. Now let's consider a packet of butterscotch Angel Delight from 1988, 20 years on. First, the ingredients:

INGREDIENTS: Sugar, Modified Starch, Vegetable Oil (Hydrogenated), Emulsifiers (Propylene Glycol Monostearate, Lecithin), Gelling Agents (Disodium Monostearate, Sodium Pyrophosphate), Caramel, Caseinate, Lactose, Whey Powder, Flavourings, Salt, Colours (Annatto, Canthaxanthin).

A casual glance would indicate there hasn't been that much change. A casual glance would be wrong. First, the list is much longer and more detailed, explaining the function of several ingredients. From this you could deduce that people are now anxious to know exactly what goes into their food and why. Secondly, the word 'artificial' has disappeared. Indeed, on the front of today's packet is the bold legend 'No Artificial Colours or Preservatives'. We will sidestep a rather semantic discussion as to what can and cannot legitimately be described as artificial, and observe that there has clearly been a public reaction against artificiality in food. Below the recipe idea on the back you can now read the following:

'As well as being free from preservatives, Angel Delight now only contains colours like those found in nature. It is a delicious treat which, in a well balanced diet, provides all the goodness you expect from a dessert made with milk. If preferred, Angel Delight tastes just as nice when made with skimmed milk.'

So, a reaffirmation of the point about artificial colours followed by dietary information. Clearly many people are now concerned about how balanced their diet is (what quantities of Angel Delight belong in a balanced diet is another issue we will sidestep). People are also trying to cut down their fat intake by using skimmed milk. That times really have changed is strongly reinforced by a table which also appears on the back of the packet:

ANGEL DELIGHT NUTRITION INFORMATION				
As consumed per serving	Fat: g	Protein: g	Carbohydrate: g	Energy calories
Whole Milk	6.1	2.9	16.3	127
Skimmed Milk	3.3	3.0	16.5	104

This table would have been unthinkable in 1968. The general theory behind it is that provision of information leads to choice, and choice leads to self-determination. But many would argue that that is just a pipe dream. Will people actually be able to plan their diet using this dietary information? Do they know enough to interpret the information against an ideal diet, and judge the goodness of what they are eating? A film report we made in the last series of *Food and Drink* provides an interesting answer.

We followed a group of diabetics around a supermarket in Aylesbury. They were led by Norma McGough, a dietician from Aylesbury Diabetics Clinic. Diet, of course, is crucial to diabetics and Norma was teaching her group how to use the self-same information quoted above to regulate their intake of carbohydrates, fats and so on. In a very short time we saw perfectly ordinary people with no more than the average knowledge of food take control of their own diets. And they didn't have to walk around *all* day long with a calculator. Maurice Hanssen, author of the *E for Additives* books, watched the film in our studio and said, 'I thought it was simply splendid, not just because of what the diabetics are doing but because of the example it gives all of us. We can all do just as they did – go out, look at the labels, read the ingredients, learn about food and actually eat for health.'

The final observation we should make about the Angel Delight packets concerns the very interesting phase that product labelling went through in the eighties – the introduction of E numbers. The EEC brought these in to indicate approval of their use as being safe. Manufacturers were given the choice of either naming the substance or substituting the appropriate E number in its place. Among the E numbers that could be found on the 1988 packet are:

E 322 (Lecithin)
E 150 (Caramel)
E 160b (Annatto)
E 161g (Canthaxanthin)

But in fact, not a single E number now appears. General Foods confirm that they did display E numbers initially but discovered public hostility to them. Far from regarding E numbers as indications of safety, people began to judge products with no E numbers as good, and products containing several E numbers as bad. General Foods and many other manufacturers have now reverted to naming the ingredients in full.

Some would bemoan public ignorance in misinterpreting the whole point of E numbers, but the episode shows that people began to judge how highly processed and artificial products were by counting the number of Es contained – not a bad rule of thumb. And the public's hostility reflected a genuine reaction against highly processed, ersatz foods.

Many captains of the food industry are bitter about the recent campaigns against additives, and no doubt feel that a little knowledge is a dangerous thing. But I and the *Food and Drink* team feel that a little knowledge is only a stepping stone on the path to greater knowledge. People learned to use telephone books, railway timetables and computer manuals. (Some of us even do our own VAT returns!) In years to come, we will also achieve a much greater understanding of food and diet. It will not be a Utopia of vegetarians and *Guardian* readers where the packet and the tin are unheard of. Good-quality convenience products will continue to sell alongside fresh foods – and with the fresh foods we will cook for the sheer enjoyment of it.

More than once, experts on *Food and Drink* have warned that by the end of the century, food technology will have totally deskilled us. They paint a grim picture of a solitary figure, hunched in front of a microwave, with no conception of 'the family meal'. It doesn't *have* to happen; indeed, we show every sign of taking control of our diet. And using the wide selection of recipes in this book is as good a start as any.

From low-cost budget cooking to tempting fish recipes; from excellent ideas for meats to filling fuel foods; from puddings to American specialities – the whole range of Michael's 'crafty cooking' is here. Jill pursues and finds real tea and coffee, she has excellent advice on making orange squash, ginger beer and homemade wine, and she has written a practical chapter about enjoying wine. (Don't miss out on her wine tips for some of Michael's recipes.) Chris, meanwhile, has been travelling the length and breadth of Britain in search of food stories. He visits a roadside 'grubwagon' in Yorkshire, the kitchen of a Michelin-starred confectioner and chef in Cambridge, an ice-cream maker in Somerset and a lunch club in South London. In addition, he profiles the finalists in our Supercook '88 competition, who then present their own winning recipes.

Whether you want to buy wine or make it, whether you want a vegetarian Christmas dinner or a magical way of carving a turkey, whether you want cheap simple snack ideas or spectacular dishes for a special occasion . . . we have something here for you. Bon appétit!

Peter Bazalgette
Producer of *Food and Drink*

May, 1988

A REFRESHING CUPPA

REAL TEA AND COFFEE
JILL GOOLDEN

If a thumbnail sketch of the typical British character were to be drawn, prominent among the attributes would be our national passion for the good old British 'cuppa'. Can't you see it? 'Typical Brit: plays cricket; watches football; eats fish and chips; greatest love of all, a cup of tea.'

Our continuing love affair with that vital, spirit-cheering leaf began during the reign of Elizabeth I, when the first British galleons buffeted their way back from the earliest expeditions to China. The first packets of tea cost an exorbitant £6 to £10 each, but even this steep price was not enough to put us off; 'China Tcha', 'Tay' or 'Tee' quickly gained the reputation for being 'wholesome, preserving perfect health until extreme old age and good for clearing the sight' (well, certainly better than gin, at any rate).

And today we still think of it as thirst-quenching, (frequently) delicious, giving a slight lift with its caffeine content and perking up the appetite with its trace of tannin. Add to this the ritual of making a good cup, and the sociable aspect of enjoying it with friends, and there you have it; the perfect drink.

Tea was not the first hot, dark drink fortified with caffeine and tannin to catch our imaginations. It was narrowly pipped at the post by coffee which made it to England about seven years earlier, and indeed the famous Tudor Coffee Houses (Samuel Pepys' notorious haunts) were the first places where tea was publicly sold. But the coffee habit took many centuries to catch on in England. Unlike our neighbours on the Continent, we did not immediately become a nation of coffee-drinkers.

It seems, though, that coffee is now going to have its day. The gap in popularity between coffee and tea is closing all the time and although still not considered *quite* so British and not *quite* so typical, coffee now warms millions of British hearts each day. Perhaps our thumbnail sketch should go on 'universal office mainstay, 10 cups of coffee a day'.

But although tea and coffee are virtually our national drinks, it is surprising how little we know about them, and especially how little we know about getting the best out of them. Take tea, for instance. The tea bag was first invented in the early fifties by Tetley, and its popularity has steadily grown and grown. Sales of tea bags now outnumber loose leaves by three to one.

The teas blended to produce (so their makers believe) the perfect cup from the bag may vary quite considerably from the teas blended to make a fine cup of leaf tea. Gradually, our tastes have altered, nudged along by the tea-bag trend. In short, there has been a minor revolution, and convenient and splendid though tea-bag tea may be, we are perhaps in danger of losing an art, a part of our heritage.

REAL TEA

Tea comes in no less than 1,500 different flavours, although most of us limit our experience to a measly one, probably our favourite tea bag. There is only one sort of tea plant, which originated in China and parts of India, but due to the different types of soils, climates and altitudes in the 25 countries where it is now grown, many different types of tea have evolved. The differences in scents, strengths and flavours are quite considerable and it is only recently that I have discovered them for myself.

During the *Food and Drink* Summer Quiz, when Oz Clarke and I had to pit our taste-buds against each other in a nerve-racking tasting competition, one of the subjects to come up was tea. I was fully aware that this wasn't my strong point, so before the great combat took place, I whistled round the local shops, buying the best-known 'speciality' teas, so that I could get in a bit of practice. And the tasting I set up in my kitchen opened the door on a totally new pleasure in life.

Here are some of my tasting notes:

Lapsang Souchong
Very dark, black China tea with elongated leaves before the water is poured – prone to 'strangers' (for the information of the tea-bags-only brigade, a 'stranger' is a straight rod of tea which floats on the surface like a short stick). Makes a very pale tea, rather wishy-washy looking. The scent is powerfully smoky and fragrant in a clean, refreshing way, and the scent carries over into the smoky flavour.

Earl Grey
Traditionally a blend of China and Darjeeling teas flavoured with the citrus oil of bergamot. Gives a pale, insipid-looking cup of tea, but don't be fooled by appearances! Highly scented, almost pungent with a refreshing mild taste. A marvellous compromise between the pale and weak China tea, and the darker and stronger Indian tea. For a 'beefier' brew, more Indian tea could be added.

Assam
A blend from Northern India, with good colour, a slightly malty character, 'full-bodied' and thick, but gentle – no harsh components, and smooth. A good tea for convinced tea-baggers to cut their teeth on.

Darjeeling
Another Northern Indian tea, from the Himalayan foothills. Known as 'the champagne of teas' and attributed with a grape-like aroma. Light-brown tea in colour, with a delicious, fresh, zingy flavour, slightly 'green' tasting – reminds you of bendy twigs and saplings.

Ceylon
Makes another pale-brown tea with a lovely flowery, fragrant aroma. Has an attractive citrusy freshness and a hint of the flavour of flowers. Many flavours harmoniously combined like a 'potpourri'.

Kenya
Makes a bright, copper-coloured tea with body and guts, and a harsh 'coppery' taste. Rather a bitter, coarse flavour, very tannic (the element that makes the edges of your tongue curl up). Because it gives such instant colour and body, Kenyan tea forms a major part of most tea-bag blends.

I tasted a great number of different tea-bag teas, travelling around the countryside during a cold spell in January when I was judging the 'grubwagon' competition sponsored by the *Sun* newspaper (see p.55). For convenience, tea bags are almost invariably used in the wagons, and sometimes produce pretty dreadful results. But it should be simple to make a good single cup of tea, I convinced myself on return, and set about trying to find out how.

A single cup of tea

To enjoy a single 'cuppa' without resorting to the anonymity of the tea bag, try a tea infuser. This egg-shaped device, like a double teaspoon, allows you to make a single cup of tea, using the speciality tea of your choice.

Variously called 'tea balls', 'tea eggs', 'mesh infusers' and 'spoon tea infusers' they can cost anything from £0.70 to £2, or if you really take your tea seriously you could buy an antique silver one for £200! They are available from most kitchen shops, from speciality tea shops and from many department stores. The rules are simple:

1 Half-fill one side of the infuser (say, a generous half-teaspoonful). You must allow room for the hot water to circulate around the leaves, especially since they swell while infusing. Place the infuser in a cup or mug.
2 Use fresh, boiling water, and pour over the infuser in the cup.
3 The tea will infuse quickly. You can aid it by stirring the infuser in the water. The period of immersion depends on how strong you like your tea.
4 Use a leaf tea, as the 'dust' used in tea bags could escape through the holes of the infuser.

Speciality teas seem expensive to buy, but we tested the economy of tea infusers and were pleasantly surprised. We got 110 cups from a standard 125-gram packet, resulting in tea at ½ pence a cup. A quick calculation revealed that this was *one-third* of the cost of a one-cup tea bag.

REAL COFFEE

As with tea, it repays spending time boning up on the different types of coffee available. If you know how to make the most of each type you'll definitely improve on the quality of each cup.

Nearly 90% of coffee drunk in this country is 'instant'. (A much higher ratio of the convenient 'alternative' to the real thing than you'd find anywhere else in the world, incidentally.) World trends show that in predominantly tea-drinking countries such as ours, most coffee is drunk in powder or granule form – perhaps because instant coffee tends to have a milder, less individual taste. Or maybe we're just a thoroughly lazy lot, accustomed to taking the shortest cut.

But having enjoyed hassle-free instant coffee for fifty years, we are again looking for something else; perhaps, now that our taste-buds are accustomed to the black bean, for more coffee flavour. Superior instant coffees and freeze-dried versions have become increasingly popular, and have paved the way for a return to real coffee: with its aroma, taste and satisfying deliciousness, quite a different drink.

Even if you have never tasted coffee made from fresh ground beans, either ready-ground or freshly milled, you will more than likely have walked past a proper coffee merchant's shop and smelt the enticingly marvellous aroma of real coffee. Even wheeling your trolley down the aisle in a good supermarket where you can grind your own beans, you may have caught a faint waft of the inviting – and unique – smell of roasting coffee.

The coffee tree – for convenience in harvesting, generally pruned down to a manageable bush – originated in Africa. The name 'coffee' may stem from the Arabic word 'kaweh', meaning strength or vigour, or from 'Kaffa', the province of Ethiopia where the plants were thought to have originated. The seeds are the crucial bit; these hard, lozenge-shaped beans are encased in a fleshy fruit, which is discarded when the crop is first picked. Before being ground, the beans are roasted until they are light to dark brown, glistening with natural oil and deliciously aromatic.

Most coffee beans are sold already roasted; you can roast the greeny-grey natural beans yourself, but it is probably better done professionally, since the beans should ideally be tossed in the air throughout their high-temperature baking to achieve an even roast. (Coffee merchants use a rotating roasting cylinder.)

If you are determined to experiment, top restaurateur Nico Ladenis of Simply Nico promises that you can achieve good results – and certainly the freshest coffee you can get – by roasting your own beans. Use a roasting tray, with the beans spread well out in a single layer. Roast for 15 to 20 minutes in a very hot oven, for a light roast (higher in caffeine, he maintains); 20 to 25 minutes for a medium roast. Most coffee merchants offer four different levels of roast, and even ready-ground, pre-packed coffee will have some indication on the pack of the level of the roast.

The best guide to the level of roast is the colour of the beans. 'Light' or 'pale' roast beans are likely to have a mild flavour, are generally drunk with milk, and may be described as 'breakfast blends'. 'Medium' roast beans make stronger coffee with a fuller flavour. A full roast gives the beans a dark mahogany colour and imparts a strong, bitterish flavour (much loved in Latin countries); it is generally drunk without milk. 'Dark' roast beans (continental, or after-dinner coffee) are the strongest: dark, bitter and generally drunk black.

The strength of the roast, however, is not the only variable; different coarsenesses of grounds call for different methods of preparation. Filters, such as an inverted plastic cone lined with special filter paper, require finely ground or 'filter fine' coffee, but a jug works better with much coarser grounds. The 'plunger' or 'cafetière' method (see below) takes medium grounds. Espresso machines, either those in Italian restaurants and cafés or the small, portable ones coffee addicts have in their kitchens at home, take extremely fine grounds. Thick, sweet Turkish or Greek coffee calls for pulverised grounds. If, for perfect freshness, you grind coffee beans yourself, there are numerous gadgets, both manual and electric, available. Grind the beans for a short time for coarse grounds, or longer for fine grounds.

Making real coffee is actually no more of an effort than using tea leaves to brew a cup of tea. Admittedly, to make tea, there is only one piece of standard equipment – the pot – whereas all manner of pots (both electric and manual) and other paraphernalia can be used for making coffee. But they are not essential; you can make a perfect cup of real coffee with just an ordinary jug, a sieve and a tea strainer. When Nico Ladenis joined me in a coffee-tasting in the studio – testing the different methods for taste, incidentally, not the individual coffees – we decided that the simplest, most basic method of making fresh coffee in a jug came up with the best results.

The perfect jug of coffee

Use ground coffee that is as fresh as possible.

The coffee should be coarsely ground and of a medium to dark roast.

1 Warm the jug.

2 Use 4 or 5 dessertspoons of coffee per pint of water (you can, of course, make it stronger if you prefer).

3 Fill the kettle with fresh, cold water (i.e. run the tap for a minute beforehand).

4 Add the water when it has just come off the boil.

5 Stir well and leave for 3 minutes.

Some aficionados swear by a wooden spoon for stirring; others recommend dropping 2 or 3 teaspoons of cold water on the grounds at the surface to make them sink. If the grounds have sunk when you serve the coffee, you may not need to strain it. Warm or hot milk preserves the temperature of the coffee. And one last tip – *never* reheat coffee, if you value flavour at all.

If you still think that making real coffee is a hassle, hang on, please, because you can buy the right coffee for your needs ready packed in vacuum-sealed containers in the supermarket or delicatessen – even if you only want the occasional single cup. At home, I rely on well-kept coffee bags, containing ground coffee and used much like a tea bag, but there are all sorts of other crafty methods for packing the flavour and aroma of real coffee into a single cup. We confronted a brave team of compulsive coffee drinkers with ten methods for making a single cup of real coffee and asked them to compare their ease of use, efficiency and the taste of the end product.

Dismissed were such oddities as a 'coffee sock' (literally a stockinette sock supported on a wire ring) on the grounds of a poor end result, and the difficulty of good washing-up; a slow and inconvenient upside-down Neapolitan pot, with difficult-to-follow instructions; and a metal coffee filter which needs insulated hands – and possibly a screwdriver – to operate. Four methods passed the test on the strength of convenience and simplicity: the coffee bag (sold in vacuum-sealed packs), the one-cup coffee filter (sold in a stack, each filter ready-charged with sufficient coffee for a single cup), the cafetière (a glass jug with an integral filter on a plunger which separates the grounds within the jug, once brewed) and the ordinary kitchen jug, plus spoon and tea strainer.

I have to admit, devoted as I am to the coffee bag, that the jug, closely followed by the cafetière, won the day, though only narrowly.

Unlike instant coffee, real coffee grounds can quickly go stale once the packet is opened. Grinding beans yourself as and when you need them is one solution, but even ready-ground coffee can be kept quite fresh in an airtight container, and preferably in a cool place, such as the refrigerator. A great tip for the milder roasts, however, is to keep your real coffee (beans or grounds) in the freezer, and simply use it as you would normally – no thawing necessary. As for coffee bags – on which I now count myself an expert – they should also be kept in an airtight container. But the key tip is to use them up quickly so that turnover is rapid. Otherwise, they soon become stale and flavourless.

BUDGET IDEAS

INTRODUCTION
CHRIS KELLY

In Britain today, Gingerbread men (outside the baker's shop) are greatly outnumbered by Gingerbread women. The Gingerbread organisation was founded by Tess Fothergill in 1970 to help single-parent families. There are currently about a million such families, 89% are headed by women, and Gingerbread's 13,000 members now form some 300 autonomous self-help groups throughout the country. We visited the Peckham branch, which meets at the Bird in Bush Community Centre in the Old Kent Road in South London, because we had heard something interesting was cooking.

For details of your nearest Gingerbread group, contact:
Gingerbread Head Office
35 Wellington Street
London WC2E 7BN

Telephone: 01-240 0953

Funded by the Catholic Children's Society, but run on strictly non-sectarian lines, the Centre itself is a remarkable success story. As well as providing a meeting place for Gingerbread, the Project Leader, Pat Hennessy, has encouraged volunteers to set up adult and toddler groups; play groups; family drop-ins; literacy, photography and keep-fit classes; discussions and holiday projects. These schemes get the fantastic local support they deserve.

The Peckham Gingerbread group has fifteen or so members. Mostly, when they get together at the Bird in Bush, they talk about the problems of adjusting to single parenthood, but they also plan social events. Budgets are tight. An occasional big night out, such as a trip to a Sinatra concert, brightens the routine but makes a large hole in the kitty, so the Gingerbread mothers have devised an entertainment that only costs £1 a head. One Sunday every month, two of them cook lunch for the rest, including children.

Sabira Jaffer is one of the group's most creative chefs. Born in Tanzania, she came to Britain when she was sixteen. What was her first impression of British food? 'I couldn't taste it,' she says. There's no danger of the Sunday club making that complaint about her dishes. Sabira uses spices imaginatively in her own blend of East African and English cuisine. The result is tasty, nutritious and cheap: three qualities dear to the heart of Richard Shepherd, executive chef at Langan's Brasserie, the most written-about restaurant in London. In *Food and Drink*'s latest challenge, we invited him to join the Peckham group one weekend and give them the benefit of his experience. It's a measure of Richard's realistic approach to cuisine that he was quite prepared to learn from Sabira and her friends. He was able to identify with them: 'It took me back to my days of having to watch the pennies.'

Returning the favour, Richard later invited his hostesses to be his guests at Langan's. They arrived looking a million dollars. 'It was so grand,' said Sabira, 'but he made us feel really special. He's a lovely person.' Afterwards the party moved on to Stringfellows night club, where they stayed until 3 am. As a memento, Richard presented the Bird in Bush Centre with a microwave. Among other things, it has proved immensely useful for heating the babies' milk. 'I don't know how we managed without it,' says Sabira.

Few of Britain's leading chefs would have related so well to the Peckham group. Weston-super-Mare, Richard's birthplace, is not prominent among the world's gastronomic high spots. Its cuisine, like its beach, is 'relatively featureless', but it was holiday jobs in Weston's cafés that gave Richard a taste for cooking. His mind was made up by the time he was twelve. Even then he knew he could do better than the chefs he watched.

The first essential for his ten-year plan was a move to London, and, at eighteen, he became a trainee at Simpson's-in-the-Strand at a salary of £8.50 per week: live out, provide your own uniform. The next step was the old Savoy Grill under the great Trompetto: 'disciplined; iron fist; always immaculate. He had the tallest hat I've ever seen on a chef.' Shepherd was much impressed when the master's white jackets came back from the laundry, not folded, like those of ordinary mortals, but laid lovingly in a box, on tissue paper.

Next stop was the Grand Hotel du Cap Ferrat. When he set out, Shepherd didn't know where the French Riviera was. Broke (he sold his camera and second-hand radio to pay the fare), and not speaking a word of the language, he travelled hopefully. Despite a drop in wages to £21 a month, the move paid off. At the end of the season he transferred to La Réserve de Beaulieu, further down the coast towards Nice. It was there he met his wife, Christine. Returning to London, he worked at the Dorchester and the Capital Hotel in Knightsbridge (gaining a Michelin star on the way) before joining Peter Langan at Langan's Brasserie. Just over a decade later, he now heads a staff of 100 catering daily for 600 covers.

Richard's dream is to run a little place in the country, just a modest 40-seater, which is 'paid for, lock, stock and barrel', but which he doesn't have to rely on to make a living. It would be somewhere to experiment, beyond the reach of gossip columns and the tremendous pressures of mass catering. That's the great thing about dreams.

Until then, firmly pinned to reality, Richard Shepherd never stops learning. His two hours spent in a Peckham kitchen reminded him that good, flavoursome food needn't cost West End prices, and gave enormous pleasure to the mothers of Gingerbread.

SABIRA JAFFER'S
SPICY CHICKEN WITH MUSHROOM SAUCE
Serves 4

1 small chicken, cut into 4 joints
1 teaspoon garam masala
(alternatively, make your own by mixing ground cardamom, coriander,
ground cloves, ground black pepper and salt)
Chicken stock made with chicken bones, ½ onion, chopped, 1 carrot,
chopped, 1 bay leaf (or use a stock cube if preferred)
A little butter
½ onion, chopped
4-6 oz (100-175 g) mushrooms, washed and sliced
¼ pint (150 ml) natural yoghurt

Skin the joints and place in a casserole dish. Sprinkle with garam masala and refrigerate for 4 to 6 hours to marinate.

Meanwhile, put the chicken bones in a saucepan, add the chopped half onion, carrot, bay leaf and 2 to 3 pints (1.2 to 1.75 litres) water. Bring this to the boil and then simmer for 2 to 3 hours.

Pre-heat the oven to 425°F (220°C), gas mark 7. Bake the chicken in the casserole dish for 35 to 40 minutes. After cooking, carefully strain off the fat and add the remaining juices to the chicken stock. Keep warm.

Sweat the chopped onion till clear in a little butter. Add the washed, sliced mushrooms and continue to sweat.

Strain the chicken stock into a small pan and reduce to ¼ pint (150 ml) over a fierce heat. Season and pour the chicken stock over the onion and mushrooms and bring to the boil. Add the yoghurt at the last minute. Cover each piece of chicken with the sauce and serve with pilau rice.

PILAU RICE
Serves 4

1 onion
1 cup long grain rice
1 bay leaf
Salt and pepper to taste

Slice onion and place in a large casserole, with the bay leaf. Add the rice and double the quantity of water, and bring to the boil. Season, cover with greased paper and lid, and cook for 15 minutes in a hot oven at 425°F (220°C), gas mark 7. Remove the lid and cover, and lightly break up the rice with a fork before serving.

RICHARD SHEPHERD'S APPLE PIE
Serves 6

You can use frozen shortcrust pastry for this, for convenience, or make your own. The addition of the orange creates a very unusual, deliciously tangy flavour.

1 large packet frozen shortcrust pastry
1½ lb (750 g) cooking apples, peeled, cored and sliced
1 orange, peeled and divided into segments
A little milk to glaze

Pre-heat the oven to 350°F (180°C), gas mark 4. Divide the pastry in two. Roll out one half thinly and line a pie plate with it. Trim the edges. Put the sliced apples and a layer of orange segments on the pastry, sprinkle with a little sugar to taste. Roll out the rest of the pastry to make a lid, lay it on top and crimp the edges. Brush with the milk and bake for approximately 25 to 30 minutes until golden brown.

RECIPES
MICHAEL BARRY

Age Concern's tips on budget shopping

These tips were specially developed for *Food and Drink* by Age Concern following a feature on menus for senior citizens. They will help you choose good, fresh food, especially if you are living on a pension.

- Plan your meals for a few days ahead with a shopping list.

- Choose basic and unprocessed foods which are cheaper: oats instead of branded cereals, for example, or a bacon hock instead of veal and ham pie.

- Supermarket 'own brands' are cheaper, if you can get to a supermarket. (Some now offer free transport.)

- Check the weight against the price on the packet. Sometimes smaller packs on special offer work out cheaper.

- Avoid gimmicky packaging or food sold in special health or festive sections; they usually have a higher mark-up.

- Markets are good for low-cost, fresh food, but insist on quality.

- Learn the days and times that perishables like chicken, fish and dairy products are reduced for quick sale, but they must be eaten at once.

- Look for broken pieces and offcuts of ham, bacon or cheese. Many butchers and grocers sell them cheaply.

- Cheapest is not always the best. Lean mince and low-fat sausages can be better value, as well as being healthier, as they contain more meat.

- Sharing large amounts with neighbours or friends saves money, particularly with vegetables from the market, and cereals.

VEGETARIAN NUT WELLINGTON
Serves 4

I am indebted to Rose Elliot, the vegetarian cookery author, and to one of her ardent fans, for the idea behind this nut-cutlet with pretensions. The fan, a friend, makes this on high days and holidays. It's quite scrumptious and grand enough for the poshest do, though it fits a very modest pocket! I suggested it as a dish for vegetarians at Christmas and the response from them (and quite often from their non-vegetarian spouses) was tremendous. Vegetarian puff pastry (still a little unusual) is available from selected supermarkets. It contains no animal fats.

11 oz (300 g) vegetarian puff pastry
1 small onion
2 celery stalks
2 garlic cloves
1 tablespoon oil
4 oz (100 g) walnuts
4 oz (100 g) cashew nuts
4 oz (100 g) brazil nuts
6 oz (175 g) chestnut purée
2 eggs
1 heaped teaspoon paprika
1 teaspoon oregano
2 tablespoons lemon juice
Salt and pepper
2 oz (50 g) button mushrooms, wiped clean
Beaten egg to glaze

Roll out the pastry and line a 2-lb (1-kg) oblong loaf tin, leaving enough overlapping on either side to cover the top. Peel, chop and fry the onion, celery and garlic in a little oil. Put in a bowl with all the remaining ingredients except the mushrooms. Mix well and bind together with the eggs. Put the mushrooms into the bottom of the lined loaf tin and then fill the tin with the mixture, pressing it down firmly to fill the spaces in between the mushrooms. Brush the pastry edges with a little beaten egg to seal, and cover the pie with the overlapping pastry. Trim the edges.

Put a baking sheet on top of the loaf tin and turn over. Carefully remove the loaf tin. Decorate the loaf with pastry leaves, make a few cuts in the pastry, and brush it lightly with beaten egg.

Pre-heat the oven to 425°F (220°C), gas mark 7. Cook the loaf for about one hour. Halfway through the cooking, reduce the temperature to 350°F (180°C), gas mark 4.

CHICKEN LIVER PILAU
Serves 4

All over the rich culinary triangle that stretches between Cairo, Istanbul and Delhi you can find versions of this simple and subtle dish, combining delicately spiced rice and pungent morsels of liver. The name changes from pilau to polo to biriani, and the methods vary slightly too. This is the crafty one. Serve with a green salad and a lemonette dressing (see below).

1 lb (450 g) chicken livers, carefully washed
1 small onion, finely chopped
1 clove of garlic, peeled and chopped
1 tablespoon each butter and oil
8 oz (225 g) long grain rice
2 tablespoons currants
A pinch of saffron (optional)
1 tablespoon garam masala

Sauté the livers, onion and garlic in the butter and oil for 5 minutes. Remove and keep the livers. Sauté the rice and currants in the same pan until the rice becomes translucent, then add 1 pint (600 ml) water. Dissolve the saffron in half a cup of hot water, if using, and add to the rice. Season, cover and simmer for 10 minutes. Stir the livers and garam masala together and place on top of the rice. Simmer another 8 to 10 minutes, or until all the liquid is absorbed. Mix the liver well into the rice before serving.

GREEN SALAD WITH LEMONETTE DRESSING

Choose any of the enormous range of salad greens available these days: oak leaved, iceberg and mini-cos lettuces in the summer; radicchio and frilly lettuces in the autumn; and Chinese leaves, chicory and endive in the winter and spring. Aim to vary flavour and texture as well as colour. Wash, tear into small pieces and put in a salad bowl. Dress the salad just before you serve it, and toss it thoroughly.

For the lemonette dressing:
Juice of ½ lemon
½ teaspoon salt
1 teaspoon caster sugar
½ cup of olive or other salad oil

Whisk or liquidise all the ingredients until thick and pour over the salad so that the leaves are coated. Serve immediately.

Herby Lemonette
To the basic dressing add:

1 tablespoon chopped fresh parsley
1 tablespoon chopped fresh chives
1 pinch each dried basil and oregano
Leave for at least ½ hour before serving.

Oriental Dressing
To the basic dressing add:

1 tablespoon soy sauce
½ crushed clove garlic
1 teaspoon crushed fresh ginger
(or ½ teaspoon powdered ginger)
Serve straightaway.

PASTITION
Serves 4 to 6

A cross between a moussaka and a lasagne, Pastition is typical of the interlocking influences of eastern Mediterranean cooking. It is a superbly economical dish, quite capable of feeding six hungry people. The Greeks, originators of this recipe, are great pasta eaters, although they tend to like their macaroni cooked softer and in shorter, fatter lengths than the Italians, and that's exactly how it is here. Lamb is the more authentic meat, but beef will do very well.

1 lb (450 g) short cut macaroni
1 lb (450 g) lamb or beef mince
2 tablespoons oil
1 lb (450 g) peeled, chopped onions
1 × 14-oz (400-g) tin tomatoes
4 tablespoons thick tomato purée
1 teaspoon each oregano, basil and thyme
10 fl oz (300 ml) plain yoghurt
2 eggs

Pre-heat the oven to 350°F (180°F), gas mark 4.

Cook the macaroni in a pan of boiling water for 10 minutes, drain and rinse. Fry the meat in the oil until it browns and crumbles. Add the onions, tomatoes and tomato purée, stir and season with the herbs. Simmer for 20 minutes. Place the meat mixture in a baking dish and cover with the drained pasta. Mix the yoghurt and the eggs thoroughly and spoon over the pasta to cover.

Bake for 30 minutes or until the top is golden brown. Serve in wedges like a pie. It can be made in advance and reheated.

A WORD ABOUT POTATOES

Potatoes are our most eaten and least valued vegetable. They still remain the best budget food of all. It is only very recently and because of legislation that retailers have begun to name the variety you are buying. Don't make the mistake of thinking it doesn't matter – it does! Varieties of potato differ in taste at least as much as apples, and they have widely varying cooking characteristics. The following guide is not totally comprehensive, but it includes the varieties most widely available.

King Edward
Good for roasting, mashing and making chips: the most versatile. Particularly good for making chips, as they absorb slightly less fat.

Maris Piper
Particularly good for making chips, as they absorb slightly less fat.

Desirée
Best for roasting and baking.

Cara
Best for baking, as they have a neat shape and good size.

Wilja
Boiling potatoes that keep their shape well.

Estima
Boiling, particularly good in potato salads.

Romano
Good for mashing and for boiling in their skins.

The Pentlands
A prefix for a number of varieties, but all of them are good for boiling and mashing.

CRAFTY MASHED POTATOES
Serves 4

2 lb (1 kg) King Edward or Romano potatoes
4 fl oz (120 ml) hot milk
1 oz (25 g) butter
½ teaspoon ground nutmeg
Salt and pepper

Peel the potatoes, cut them evenly and boil until completely soft but not disintegrated. Drain thoroughly and allow to dry in the warm saucepan with the lid off for 2 minutes. Add the warm milk and mash thoroughly. When smooth, add the butter, nutmeg and seasoning. Whip vigorously until the mash is light and fluffy. Serve immediately.

POMMES DUCHESSE
Serves 4

1½ lb (750 g) mashed potato (see above)
1 egg
Butter for greasing

Beat the egg into the potatoes and allow to cool. Fill a piping bag with the mixture and fit with a large star nozzle. Pipe twirls approximately 2 in (5 cm) in diameter onto a greased baking tray. (These twirls can be kept in a fridge for up to 12 hours until needed.) Bake for 10 to 20 minutes in a hot oven, 400°F (200°C), gas mark 6.

CHAMP
Serves 4

1 lb (450 g) mashed potato (see above)
2 tablespoons finely chopped spring onion
4 tablespoons *fromage frais*

Stir the spring onion into the hot mash, and arrange in nests on individual plates. Make a well in the middle of each nest and fill with a tablespoon of *fromage frais*. Serve immediately.

CHIPS
Here are just a couple of hints for producing non-greasy, super-crisp chips:

1 Use clean or filtered oil.

2 Get the oil hot but not smoking.

3 Cut, wash, and drain the chips in advance so there is no excess moisture to make the oil foam.

4 Cook until pale brown, and drain.

5 Let the oil regain its temperature (about 1 minute).

6 Put the chips back in for about 45 seconds. Drain, season and serve.

BAKED POTATOES

The great trick with baked potatoes is to push a thick metal skewer through the length of each potato after you have scrubbed them. This will conduct heat to the centre of the potato, so that the inside is baked before the outside dries out. Devices with four or six prongs to hold the potatoes are available instead if you prefer.

PERFECT ROAST POTATOES

1 Make sure all the peeled potatoes are the same size.

2 Cover with water, bring to the boil and simmer for 8 minutes.

3 Drain and turn in two tablespoons of oil heated in a roasting pan in the oven.

4 Roast for approximately 45 minutes, turning once, in an oven set to 375°F (190°C), gas mark 5. Very large ones will need longer.

BREW-IT-YOURSELF!

COUNTRY AND KIT WINES

JILL GOOLDEN

One of the little-known facts of life is that home-made wine makes you happy: not merely merry (although that as well), but richly contented and comfortable. It might be that making and drinking country and kit wines imbues you with an overwhelming sense of happiness...or that only overwhelmingly happy people make country wines. Whatever it is, it's an intoxicating ingredient of most home-made wine circles.

When I was invited to judge the Grand Tournament between two rival neighbouring wine circles – Andover, the oldest in the country, and neighbouring Enham in Hampshire – I was much struck by this wonderful sense of friendship and fun that fuels the circle meetings. Recipes were for damson and dandelion and happy families all inextricably linked. Later I was the guest at a wine circle event in Billingshurst, Sussex, and there again this radiance shone through the bananas and sloes.

Perhaps one reason why wine-making inspires such marital bliss is that it takes up so much space and time that both parties have to be fully committed to the job. Much of the kitchen will be given over to the craft, and many wine-makers have specially adapted their kitchens for the buckets and demijohns. Tour the rest of the house and you'll find the cottage industry has spilt over onto the sideboard, into the airing cupboard and under the stairs.

Country wines – that is, wines made from hedgerow fruits and flowers: nettles, dandelions, blackberries, elderberries or whatever – have undoubtedly been brewed since mankind first learned how to have a good time. More recently wine kits have been developed for those of us without the benefit of a rural education. Some country wine-makers are purists through and through and won't touch a kit – they stick firmly to their primroses and parsnips – but more often these days enthusiasts are willing to mix the two approaches. Whichever line they follow, country and kit wine-makers the length and breadth of Britain get together as often as they can in a freemasonry of their own – the wine circle. Often the best way to find a wine circle in your area is through your local gardening club (they have to grow the product first) or by asking at a home-brewing shop.

Wine circles may meet officially as often as three times a week and casually more often than that. In Andover, they also organise 'progressive dinner parties' of several courses, each being prepared by a different member, eaten in a different house, with (crucial, this) a different home-made wine. The morning of the Grand Tournament in Andover, a modest five-courser had occupied various members until 3 am.

What really counts, though, is the wine, and the fact that it can be made, fairly simply, by anyone (although Great Wines can only be made by Great Wine-makers, needless to say). All fruit contains the natural ingredients for fermenting into wine, as anyone who has ever let a fruit salad stand around for long enough knows. Inside a grape, for example, is pulp, high in fruity flavours and sugar, and in the wine-making grape varieties there's also sufficient natural acidity to give a harmonious balance to wine.

Look at a whole grape – particularly a black grape – and you will see a whitish bloom on the skin. That is yeast, which, when the grape is crushed, comes into contact with the pulp and juice inside and starts working on the sugar, eventually converting it into alcohol. Left alone in suitable conditions, crushed grapes would make themselves into wine. So would other fruit as well, although to make the sort of wine you want to drink you have to intervene in the natural process and steer it in the right direction.

All home-made wine recipes do this 'steering' quite simply for you as, of course, do the kits. A typical kit will include a plastic mixing bucket, a fermentation jar, grape concentrate, bottles, labels and corks, a funnel, and clarifying agents. (You supply your own water and sugar!) One of the cheapest complete beginner's kits around, with everything you need for your first bottles of home-made wine – including very easy-to-follow step-by-step instruc-

tions – costs less than £10 from Boots' home-brewing departments. You can, of course, buy the pieces of equipment separately
(but without the instructions!) from Boots or specialist home-brewing shops. Or you can make your own wine from scratch, that is,
from first picking the fresh fruit. Either way, the aim is to produce a
good bottle of plonk at a fraction of the cost of a bought wine,
which of course carries a high level of duty.

Although all fruit – and flowers too if you like – will make wine,
they won't all make good wine. Some simply don't taste pleasant
enough in their own right, while others are too bland. A necessary
element in wine-making is acidity – without it you end up making
something akin to fruit soup. Mike Dobson, president of the
Billingshurst Wine Circle, is very conscious of that. He aims to
make wines similar in style to commercial grape wines, such as
clarets and burgundies, but using common English fruits.

He recommends rhubarb for its acidity – enough to offset the
luscious sweetness of the fruit. Elderberries also have good acidity, coupled with high levels of tannin, the element found in black
grape skins that adds a drying bitterness to young red wines, acts
as a preservative and gives them a mellowness when they have
been kept.

Judging the Andover and Enham Grand Tournament was my
first concentrated tasting of home-made country and kit wines,
although I had tasted a fair number of commercial fruit, flower,
vegetable – even tree – wines with Fred Housego, former *Master-
mind* winner, cabbie, bon viveur and recently *Rush Hour*
presenter on Radio London, in a grand taste-off for *Food and
Drink*.

Among the commercial wines we tasted were all manner of
bottled garden (and woodland) produce: apple, gooseberry,
elderflower, wheat, meadowsweet, dandelion, the Scottish blae-
berry, and even silver birch sap. From this tasting, I definitely
decided that, to my palate, second to the wine-making grape
(unquestionably in my view the most suitable fruit for vinification),
comes the English apple, which produces delicious scents and
flavours for the taste-buds to play with.

Many fruits, especially red ones such as damson and
redcurrant, excel in making a sweeter style of wine, luscious and
voluptuous. I could not give the same praise to 'sap of silver birch'
– an adventurous ingredient for the commercial fermenting vat. I
awarded it some marks for originality, but Fred unhesitatingly
gave it a minus score.

The rich range of flavours presented by the Andover and Enham competition wines was no less challenging, but infinitely more sympathetic. I was faced with a large number of bottles – red, brown, pink, gold and white – numbered and ascribed with a class. (Even some of the classes broached new ground for me, such as the 'social' class, consisting of sweet red – and brown – wines.) But there was no mention of fruit, or whether the wine was made from fresh fruit or a kit, and certainly no indication as to which wines came from which club. It was, quite properly, a genuinely blind tasting.

The first thing I had to get to grips with was the fruity sweetness of most of the wines, rather sweeter than the general run of bought grape wines. But there were some joyous scents and flavours there, blossomy fragrances, wafts of flower-petals, hints of Parma violets. Sometimes the fruit or flower origins of the brew made their presence felt; at other times they were submerged behind a harmonious vinous blend.

I was surprised that I liked a kit wine best: Ron Hill's 'quick fermenting' apple, elderberry and redcurrant, to which he adds a secret ingredient. And because I'm an honest sort of person, I'll let you know what I said about it in my tasting notes: 'Very good vinous bouquet, like Cabernet Sauvignon [one of the classic red wine-making grapes] from the New World...' Cabernet Sauvignon, my foot! – although to be fair, redcurrants and Cabernet Sauvignon do have something in common.

We twisted poor Ron's arm to reveal his mystery weapon and we passed his secret on to five million viewers – a can of port wine concentrate to give extra body. Only a couple of pips behind Ron's kit wine in my scoring came Geoff and Mickie Wells' delicious damson (recipe on page 41), about which I wrote, redeeming myself a bit, 'shouts damson. Lovely fruit character...'

I have noticed that some home-made wines seem sugary, an undesirable feature. My tip to counteract this sugariness is to ensure that the fermentation takes place over a long period at a fairly low temperature, though perhaps not quite as long as Dave Spark of the Billingshurst Wine Circle took to ferment his crab apple wine. He started it four years ago, and allowed it to ferment over a period of a year. It is one of the most dangerous brews I have encountered; extremely alcoholic, syrupy and rich. He also managed to keep it for a good long while before opening the bottle – a feat achieved by few home wine-makers of my acquaintance. Most are unable to resist tackling the latest brew the minute the tumult of the fermentation has died down, which doesn't actually make for the smoothest wine imaginable.

So Goolden tip number two (and I do have to admit this is theoretical advice, since I have not yet had the courage to put it into practice myself and make my own wine) is to keep away from the corkscrew for as long as you can – six months at least for country wines, rising to five years for a really meaty elderberry. Many kits are designed to get you something to pour into your glass as soon as conceivably possible. A great idea, but a resting period – time for maturation – does improve the quality of the wine. Wines kept for a while allow time for all the different elements to marry and develop into a harmonious blend.

I have picked up various other tips on wine-making along the way, on your behalf – and tasted the proof that they actually work. Here, with the benefit of experience behind them (accumulated experience, I hasten to add) are some secrets to successful wine-making.

Raisins or sultanas
Add body to kit wines, or wines made from grape juice. Carton grape juice can be used, but it comes from the wrong family of grapes, with too high a ratio of sugar to acids.

Bananas
Work wonders as fining agents (clearing the wine to 'fall bright' at the end of the process). They also contribute 'woomph' and body and, if you're careful, they don't alter the flavour of the wine, whether it be rhubarb, damson, or what you will. Use 1 lb (450 g) ripe bananas (peeled weight) for a single gallon of wine, or 3 lb (1.5 kg) for 5 gallons. Chop up the bananas and boil in 1 pint (600 ml) water for half an hour. The result looks like washing-up water and smells foul but don't be discouraged; when cool, strain the liquid into the fermenting vessel before the process gets under way. Discard the banana pulp.

Elderberries
Must be brought to the boil and instantly strained from the boiling water before being fermented. This kills the wild yeasts, so the chosen yeasts specially bred for making wine can be added. Elderberries are bitter fruit and the addition of blackberries can soften the tart edge you can get in pure elderberry wine. Elderberry wine needs time to mature: 3 to 5 years is recommended.

Parsnips
Can be used as an ingredient for wine and then turn up again in the Sunday lunch. To make the wine, bring the parsnips to the boil and remove from the water straightaway. The liquid can then be used to make parsnip wine, while the parsnips themselves may either be roasted immediately, or placed in the freezer for another occasion.

Blackcurrants and redcurrants
Can also be recycled. Having made blackcurrant wine, for instance, the same pulp may be reboiled and added to other fruit – say redcurrants – with 2 lb (1 kg) sugar being added per gallon.

Carrots and other root vegetables
Can give a gingery flavour, akin to ginger wine.

Sloes
If you can find them, go well with damsons, adding a nice zest of acidity, preventing them tasting like liquid jam. You can re-use the sloes, after they have done their stuff, to make sloe gin.

One final tip: if you freeze the fruit, even just overnight, before crushing, you'll find you can get more juice out of it. To maximise the extraction even further, the Cecil Vacuum system (about £14 from home wine-making shops), originally marketed for fruit juice extraction, does a thorough job with the aid of a bicycle pump. A convenient, compact press.

GEOFF AND MICKIE WELLS' DAMSON WINE
Makes 1 gallon (around 8 bottles)
You'll need the following equipment:
2 × 2-gallon white fermenting bins or buckets
1 large wooden spoon for stirring
2 × 1-gallon demijohns
2 airlocks
A plastic funnel for decanting
Muslin for straining fruit
Green bottles and corks
1½ yards (1.35 m) clear plastic tubing
Campden tablets or Metabisulphite for sterilising

For the wine:
6 lb (2.75 kg) very ripe damsons
1 lb (450 g) over-ripe bananas
1 teaspoon pectolase (pectic enzymes)
3 lb (1.5 kg) cane sugar
1 sachet port yeast
1 teaspoon yeast nutrient

Sterilise all equipment immediately before use – don't sterilise in advance or the equipment will pick up more bacteria.

Put the damsons and peeled bananas in the fermenting bin and pour over ½ gallon of boiling water. When cooled to hand-warm, mash the fruit by hand, then add ½ gallon of cold water and stir well. Stir in the pectolase, cover tightly with a tea towel or a lid, and leave for 24 hours in a warm place.

The next day, add 1 lb (450 g) sugar, the yeast and the yeast nutrient, then stir well until the sugar is dissolved. Cover the bucket again, and leave in a warm place (an airing cupboard is ideal) for 5 days, stirring 2 to 3 times daily.

Put the remaining sugar into the second bucket, and strain the fruit mixture into this through the muslin. Let it drip through naturally; do not squeeze the muslin as this causes the wine to cloud. Pour half of the juice into each demijohn through the funnel. Fit the airlocks and keep in a warm, dark place, shaking daily to aid the fermentation. An airing cupboard is ideal, or a kitchen if the demijohns are covered with dark material to keep out the light.

When the fermentation slows down a little (around 2 to 4 weeks) taste the liquid. If it tastes too dry add 1 oz (25 g) sugar to each jar and shake it. You can repeat this a few days later, to continue fermenting the wine, but the longer you ferment it, the more alcoholic the result.

When fermentation stops and the wine clears, syphon it with the plastic tubing into a bucket, leaving the sediment at the bottom of the demijohns. (You may have to syphon the wine a second time if there is a lot of sediment and the wine is cloudy.) Generally, damson wine clears very quickly. Pour into the green wine bottles and cork. (It is important that you use green bottles rather than clear ones to keep out the light and prevent the wine discolouring.) Store the bottles in a cool, dark place on a wine rack for 12 to 18 months. If the wines are stored in too warm a place there is a danger of the corks popping out. Decant before drinking.

FISHING LINES

MAKING THE MOST OF FRESH FISH

Michael Barry

Have you recently tried to buy a Dover sole in Dover? Not easy! Or how about some Whitstable native oysters in Whitstable? Only one tiny shellfish bar has a secret supply. I'm sure the same is true of a pint of local shrimps in Morecambe Bay or a pair of bloaters in Yarmouth. The traditional fish are getting hard to find in their original homes, where they were once so common.

There are complex reasons for the decline in the supplies of local fresh fish, even in fishing ports: the immediate freezing of catches, changes in retailing patterns, government regulations and overfishing have all had their effects. The list is long and gets longer, depending on whom you talk to. There has been a change in our eating habits, with a growing liking for trout and salmon at the expense of sea fish. And lastly, there is the overwhelming dominance of the new Billingsgate market in the London Docklands, though Billingsgate, on one site or another, has controlled the sale of fish since medieval times, so in itself that's nothing new.

Last century, the first commercial passenger railway in the world connected Canterbury and Whitstable on the Kent coast. The railway was nicknamed 'The Crab and Winkle Line' from the number of people who used it to get a dish of their favourite shellfish straight from the sea. The line was a victim of the infamous Beeching cuts in the sixties, but although four inshore trawlers still fish out of Whitstable, you could not tell as much from the local shops. Only a few plaice and dabs or a codling or two are fresh from the quay. The rest of the fish has 'come down from London'.

What gives most concern, though, is that the local catch won't have gone 'up' to London in the first place. France is nearer to Whitstable than our capital is, and the French know a good thing when they see it. A regular visitor to Whitstable's narrow streets is a giant freezer lorry which loads up with fish to take it directly to the market at Boulogne. It's all the more cheering, therefore, to find somewhere on the Kent coast where this trend is being reversed.

Under the arches across from the ferry terminal at Folkestone is the Stade: an ancient word for quay. It's lined on the landward side with a staggering array of public houses and inns – the Ship, the Jubilee, the Oddfellows Arms. On the other side, in the small outer harbour, rows of fishing boats moor to unload their catch before being scrubbed down and putting to sea again. These are not the long-haul giant fishing boats of Aberdeen that can stay in Arctic waters for weeks. Here, a 35-foot boat looms large among the trawlers, but trawlers these are, fishing inshore, 'tide on tide', and bringing ashore catches of cod, sole, plaice, skate and bass. And the smaller 'potting' boats bring in their hauls of crab and whelks.

It's a successful business, built on local support. Just across the Stade is the retail shop of Folkestone Trawlers Ltd, a group of fishermen who have found a local market. Much of the daily catch is sold over the counter to local shops, 'mobile shops', or to the hundreds of personal customers who love the freshest fish in Britain. When there's a glut the extra fish may go to Billingsgate or France, and Ken Thompson, 35 years on the quay, points out that tastes have changed. There isn't the demand for bloaters that there was because 'They don't like the smell in their little flats'. A lot of the shellfish landed here goes up to London, but the stalls that line the quay, selling plates of whelks, crab and shrimps, are solid testimony to the enthusiasm of Folkestone's citizens and visitors for the local delicacy.

Terry Noakes skippers the green-sided trawler marked FE20, called *Fair Chance*. He has been fishing for 15 years, and, despite complaints about pollution, government restrictions, and the local chippies who find frozen fish more profitable than fresh, he is quietly confident. 'None of our fish is frozen and we get a premium price for the quality.' He has reason to be confident; the trawlermen's shop has just been refitted in gleaming tiles and stainless steel, and the group is adding two new stern trawlers built in England to the fleet.

Health is one reason for this increasing demand for fresh fish, but flavour and the new availability on supermarket counters play a part as well. So whether you can get down to the Stade at Folkestone, or whether Sainsbury's car park is the closest you come to the sea, the following recipes I hope may offer some ideas for making the most of our most common fish.

SOLE MEUNIÈRE

One of the simplest of all sole dishes, and still the best. Make sure you have a pan or pans big enough to cook all the fish at once. They don't improve with keeping.

Per person
1 tablespoon oil
2 tablespoons butter
1 Dover or lemon sole
2 tablespoons seasoned flour
Juice of ½ lemon
Parsley to garnish

Ask your fishmonger if you want the sole filleted, as it's a fiddly job. If it's a Dover sole, ask him to skin it as well.

Heat the oil and half the butter, dip the sole in the flour, and fry gently for 3 minutes each side if filleted, 5 if on the bone. Transfer to warm plates. Wipe the pan, then melt the rest of the butter till it stops sizzling – don't let it brown. Quickly add the lemon juice, and pour over the fish. Season, garnish with parsley and serve with new potatoes.

GOUJONS OF SOLE

Serves 2

This is a crafty way to make expensive fish go further. Serve it with tartare sauce or lemon wedges for an elegant starter or buffet dish. One fish will feed two as a main course.

1 Dover sole, filleted and skinned
Juice of ½ lemon
2 tablespoons seasoned flour
1 egg, beaten
8 oz (225 g) fresh white breadcrumbs
Oil for deep frying

Cut the fillets into very thin strips, ⅓ inch (8 mm) wide, diagonally across the grain. Soak these in the lemon juice for 5 minutes. Dip in the flour, egg and breadcrumbs in that order and fry in the oil, pre-heated to just below smoking. Cook until golden, about 4 minutes. Serve hot.

PLAICE DUGLÈRE

I have 'craftied' this classic nineteenth-century French sauce. Originally it was thickened with a *beurre manié* but it's easier, and possibly healthier, to use *fromage frais*.

4 large plaice fillets
1 oz (25 g) butter
Salt and pepper
1 tablespoon finely chopped onion
4 tablespoons finely chopped tomato, without pips
1 tablespoon lemon juice mixed with 4 tablespoons water
6 tablespoons *fromage frais*
1 teaspoon cornflour

Pre-heat the oven to 350°F (180°C), gas mark 4. Put the fish in a single layer in a buttered oven dish. Season, sprinkle over the onion, the tomato and the lemon juice and water. Cover with foil and bake for 20 minutes.

Transfer the fish onto hot plates and keep warm. Pour the cooking juices into a saucepan. Add the *fromage frais*, mixed first with the cornflour. Heat gently until thick, but do not boil. Pour over the fish and serve.

HADDOCK MOUSSE
Serves 8

Haddock is a fish vastly underrated south of the border. In Scotland they are rightly addicted to it. Haddock has a firm texture and a vivid flavour, ideal for that favourite *nouvelle cuisine* starter, a hot fish mousse sliced into elegant slivers. You can serve it hot or cold, and it's good enough served in generous slices as a main course for those who, like me, think that *nouvelle cuisine* is usually too little of a good thing. The tomato sauce, whether poured over or around it, as the *'nouvelles'* like, is a delicious addition.

1½ lb (750 g) fresh haddock, skinned and filleted
4 fl oz (120 ml) vegetable oil
4 eggs
4 oz (100 g) low-fat *fromage frais*
Juice of ½ lemon
Salt and pepper
Butter for greasing
4 oz (100 g) carrots
or
4 oz (100 g) fresh salmon
A handful of fresh parsley
A handful of fresh dill (if available)

Pre-heat the oven to 325°F (160°C), gas mark 3. Cut the haddock fillet into chunks and put into a food processor or blender with the oil, eggs, *fromage frais*, lemon juice and seasoning. Purée until smooth.

Line a 2-lb (1-kg) loaf tin with greased paper and put half the puréed mixture into this. Cut the carrots or salmon into thin strips ¼ inch (5 mm) wide. Boil the carrots, and place these, or the salmon, evenly onto the mixture in the loaf tin. Put the parsley and dill in the blender with the remaining mixture and blend until fine. Cover the carrots or salmon strips with the herb mixture and place the loaf tin in a bain marie (a baking tin half-filled with water).

Bake in the oven for 35 to 45 minutes or until set. (The runnier the consistency of the *fromage frais*, the longer it will take to set: the low-fat varieties are generally runnier than the high-fat.) Remove from the oven and turn out of the loaf tin when cool, removing the greased paper. Cut into slices and serve with tomato sauce.

TOMATO SAUCE
1 × 14-oz (400-g) tin Italian chopped tomatoes
1 teaspoon sugar
Salt
Dried basil
A pinch of pepper
2 tablespoons *fromage frais* or double cream

Mix all the ingredients, apart from the *fromage frais*. Simmer the sauce, reducing until most of the liquid has evaporated. Remove from the heat and stir in the *fromage frais* or cream.

MISUNDERSTOOD MUSSELS

Our shores grow some of the finest shellfish in the world, though pollution and carelessness have threatened many of our best sources. Mussels are still one of the cheapest delicacies we have, although those we find in the shops tend these days to come from Ireland or even Spain. What the enterprising packers from these countries calculated was that if they cleaned the shells, most of the work (and the disincentive for the cook) would be gone. The cleaned mussels come in 4½-lb (2-kg) plastic bags.

Make sure that the mussels are fresh. They should be tightly shut when bought, and any open ones that do not close when tapped sharply should be discarded, as well as those with broken or cracked shells, or loose hinges. If they haven't already been cleaned, thoroughly scrub the outside before cooking and remove the beard (see illustration). Leave for an hour or two in a bucket of clean salted water to clean them internally. Any mussel which floats to the top should be discarded.

MOULES MARINIÈRES
Serves 2 to 3

1 clove garlic, chopped
6 fl oz (175 ml) apple juice
1 quart cleaned fresh mussels
Salt and pepper
1 teaspoon cornflour
5 fl oz (150 ml) double or single cream
½ cup fresh, chopped parsley

Put the garlic, apple juice and cleaned mussels in a pan, and season. Bring to the boil, cover with a lid and simmer for 5 minutes, shaking the pan frequently. The mussels will open when cooked – discard any that do not.

Mix the cornflour into the cream, add to the pan and stir. Bring back to the boil, shake again and cook for 1 minute more. Spoon the mussels and sauce into bowls and sprinkle with the chopped parsley.

BILI BI
Serves 2 to 3
This alternative recipe for mussels is a spicy transatlantic one. What its name means, I don't know.

1 tablespoon butter
1 teaspoon curry powder
4 spring onions, cut into fine strips
1 carrot, peeled and cut into fine strips
1 quart fresh mussels
5 fl oz (150 ml) double cream

Clean the mussels carefully as above. Melt the butter in a large pan. Sprinkle in the curry powder and gently sauté for 2 minutes. Add the onions and the carrot. Cook for 2 minutes, then add the mussels and a cup of water. Bring to the boil, cover and cook over a high heat for 5 minutes. Discard any mussels that remain closed.

Transfer the mussels to a serving dish. Add the cream to the sauce in the pan and boil. Pour over the mussels and serve with plenty of warm French bread.

DRESSED CRAB
Serves 4
The shell of the crab is truly intimidating to all predators, mankind included. There isn't any quick way of cleaning a crab, though the end results make all the effort worthwhile. Crabs are usually bought ready cooked in the shell. They vary in price enormously, from £1.20 to £3.00 per lb, depending on availability, but are generally cheaper in summer. Choose a crab heavy for its size with no sound of liquid inside when you shake it. Avoid crabs with cracked or broken shells.

1 × 2-lb (1-kg) crab
Juice of ½ lemon
2 tablespoons chopped parsley and chives
4 tablespoons soft brown breadcrumbs
1-2 tablespoons mayonnaise (see below)
1 teaspoon Dijon mustard
2 hard-boiled eggs

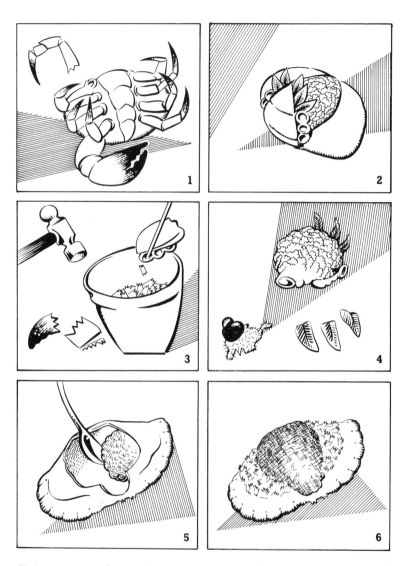

Fishmongers often sell crab they have 'dressed' themselves. If you can't get one, dress the crab yourself: twist off the legs and claws (1) and slip a knife into the horizontal black line at the back of the shell. Twist the knife and the crab will open. Pull the top and bottom apart (2) and remove the 'dead man's fingers' (the greyish-brown gills) lying on each side of the underbelly of the crab. Remove the mouth and the stomach sac behind it and discard (3). The rest is edible!

Take the brown meat from the main body of the crab and put into a bowl. Using a mallet or nutcracker, break open the claws and remove the white meat (**4**). More white meat can be found in the legs and central structure of the crab. (It does require some patience to pick all the flesh out, but is well worth it.) Put the white meat into a separate bowl and add to it the lemon juice and the parsley and chives. To the brown meat, add the breadcrumbs, mayonnaise and mustard.

Mix the ingredients in both bowls thoroughly. Pile the brown meat in the centre of the cleaned crab shell (**5**) and put a line of the white meat on either side (**6**). Decorate with the chopped, hard-boiled eggs. Serve with hot, buttered toast.

CRAFTY MAYONNAISE

This recipe produces light creamy mayonnaise, partly because whole eggs, including the more delicate whites, are used; and partly because blenders or food processors beat in extra air. You can't make this recipe without a blender or processor, but with one it's effortless.

1 whole egg
½ teaspoon salt
½ teaspoon sugar
Juice of ½ lemon
12 fl oz (350 ml) pure olive oil
(or olive and/or peanut or sunflower oil)

Put the egg, salt, sugar and lemon juice into a food processor or blender. Add a quarter of the oil and blend. Pour the remaining oil into the blender in a slow steady stream until the mayonnaise is light and creamy.

Spicy Mayonnaise
To the basic mayonnaise add:
1 teaspoon curry powder

Process again for 5 seconds.

Sauce Aurore
To the basic mayonnaise add:
1 tablespoon tomato purée
1 tablespoon chopped tomato

Process again for 5 seconds.

Mayonnaise Verte
To the basic mayonnaise add:

1 tablespoon chopped fresh parsley
1 tablespoon chopped fresh chives
1 tablespoon chopped fresh watercress

Process again for 5 seconds.

Jill Goolden carried out a tasting of the various olive oils now widely available in Britain. Basically, there are two different types:

Extra Virgin Olive Oil
Is made by cold-pressing the olives. The first pressing gives the most delicious oil, and bottles containing only this will say so. Virgin oils are generally quite rich and thick, ranging in colour from greeny-yellow to dark olive green. Their taste is powerful and so they star in dishes in which this distinctive flavour can dominate: salad dressings, ratatouille or simply trickled onto bread dried for a few minutes in a low oven (and rubbed with garlic for an extra boost). Extra virgin olive oil is relatively expensive.

Pure Olive Oil
Contains refined oil as well as fresh-pressed. It is lighter in colour, less powerful in flavour and cheaper. It is generally used for cooking meats, for frying and for making mayonnaise.

Shopping for oils
Supermarkets and grocers sell oils from Italy, Greece, Spain and France, each with their national characteristics: Tuscan (Italian) oil has a reputation for being the best; Greek is the darkest, richest, most powerfully flavoured; Spanish oil can be deliciously rich and pure (and is used by many supermarkets for their own label products); and French oil tends to be lighter in body and flavour. Prices range from £1.20 per 500 ml for oils which are the product of more than one country, to £6 per 500 ml for an estate-bottled version. In recent tastings, Safeways and Waitrose Extra Virgin oils have come out on top.

A labelling note
A new EEC agreement means that manufacturers will soon have to abide by the above definitions of 'Extra Virgin' and 'Pure'. Until then, beware the quite frequent misuse of the word 'pure'.

POTTED SHRIMPS
Serves 4

A Lancashire tradition, this is most delicious made with the tiny brown or pink Morecambe Bay shrimps. If you can't find the genuine article, frozen peeled prawns are an acceptable substitute.

4 oz (100 g) shrimps (shelled and washed fresh ones, or frozen)
2 oz (50 g) butter
¼ teaspoon allspice
¼ teaspoon mace
¼ teaspoon paprika
Sprig of fresh parsley
Wholemeal toast

Defrost the shrimps, if frozen. Melt the butter in a saucepan over a gentle flame. Add the shrimps and spices, and stir. Pour the mixture into small ramekin dishes, allow to cool, then refrigerate for 2 to 3 hours. Decorate with a sprig of parsley, and serve with small rounds of wholemeal toast.

ANCHOVIES ON TOAST

I found this recipe in an early nineteenth-century collection. I've 'craftied' it a little, but the robust combination of the strong flavours of that period survives. Use anchovies tinned in oil, as the brined fish take a lot of preparing (and getting used to).

For each serving:
2 oz (50 g) Cheshire cheese
1 oz (25 g) fresh parsley
1 slice granary bread
Butter for spreading
2 anchovy fillets

Pre-heat the grill. Grate the cheese, finely chop the parsley, and mix together. Toast the granary bread, and butter each slice carefully, making sure the whole surface is covered. Cross the anchovy fillets over on each slice of bread and cover evenly with the cheese and parsley mixture. Put onto a fire-proof plate or dish, and flash under the hot grill, till bubbling.

FILLING FOODS

INTRODUCTION
CHRIS KELLY

On Menwith Hill in the Yorkshire dales, close to Harrogate, there's a cluster of giant mushrooms. At least, that's what they look like; bulbous growths the size of a house. Allegedly they form a US listening post, and are there to tap conversations or signals which could contain useful information.

I have this fantasy that one day they might eavesdrop, not on calls criss-crossing the skywaves, but on a tiny caravan parked in a lay-by just down the road. Should this happen, American defence experts will hear something like this:

> WOMAN'S FRIENDLY VOICE: Hello love. How are you today?
> MAN'S VOICE: Not bad, ta.
> WOMAN'S FRIENDLY VOICE: Are you taking the pie and peas?
> MAN'S VOICE: Aye.
> WOMAN'S FRIENDLY VOICE: Right you are, love. That'll be 80 pence.

What would the boffins make of that? Could it be some elaborate code? An obscure reference to nuclear attack? Is 'pie and peas' spy-speak for top secret deadly weapons?

The truth is even more delicious than the fantasy. The caravan at Kettlesing on the A59 belongs to Mick and Peg Sykes. From it they serve what the *Sun* newspaper and *Food and Drink*'s Jill Goolden agreed is the best food of any grubwagon in Britain.

In the last couple of decades, I've sampled dozens of roadside tea-stalls. Standards of cleanliness and quality vary enormously, but I can hardly recall eating anything truly home-made in any of them. (I don't count sandwiches and hamburgers, which consist chiefly of commercially prepared ingredients.) So Mick and Peg's wholesome cooking came as a culture-shock.

You reach them by branching off the A1 and following the A59 through Knaresborough and Harrogate (where it's sign-posted for Skipton). Some six miles further on is your reward.

I asked Ian Howie, who drives long-distance for Vibroplant, why he keeps returning to Mick and Peg. 'It's just the best,' he said. Once drivers had little choice, and often had to put up with rotten food and worse service. 'Back then, if you asked for scrambled eggs, they'd say, "Get out, you big poof!" ' Now things have changed. 'I was in a place the other day where this bloke asked if they did boiled potatoes. "No," they said. "Right," he said, "I'll go somewhere where they do." And he left. It wouldn't have happened before.'

Ian was also adamant that there's a definite North/South divide. According to him, travellers' food in the North is better, cheaper and fills more of the plate. He castigated Little Chefs everywhere for serving portions 'only big enough for children'.

Mind you, appetites on the A59 are not what you'd call dainty. It's not uncommon for a customer to breakfast on one of Mick's Big Bites – a sausage, bacon and cheese omelette in a bun – followed by a great triangle of pie with mushy peas and a couple of Peg's scones.

When I joined Mick and Peg in their tiny caravan kitchen, every time one of them passed me, we both had to take a deep breath. Rich, homely smells tantalised from every direction. Mick had the griddle sizzling with his morning specials. Peg, warm and motherly, was taking plump home-made pies out of the oven. It was like a conjuring trick: an endless succession of pies, all brown and crusty; apple; apple and blackcurrant; steak and kidney; savoury mince and, making its debut that very day, 'Peg's Pie', made with pork and sausage meat.

There were three varieties of carrot cake, cakes made with coffee and chocolate, jam sponge with a cream filling, and a lovely fruit slab perked up with Guinness. And not one, but three, kinds of scone – big, fresh and hard to resist. A large slice of fruit pie was only 35p, and Mick's excellent, strongish tea, at 20p, was served in mugs, instead of hopeless disposable cups. This was a real meal, and amazing value for money.

How did Mick and Peg come to be perched here, overlooking the farmlands of North Yorkshire? Mick had been an asphalt layer, while Peg worked as a doctor's receptionist, picking up a little extra in the evenings as a cinema cashier. Mick, who was separated, came to the pictures regularly with his children. 'He had right sorrowful-looking eyes,' says Peg. Subsequently they bumped into each other at a dance hall, and the die was cast.

They set up in business eight years ago. At first the going was rough. The daily takings rarely amounted to more than £8 and at the end of one dreadful Saturday, there was only £1 in the till. Friends told Peg she must be mad. More determined than ever, she and Mick persevered.

Gradually the customers started to roll in, spreading the word as they covered the North. Since they won the *Sun*'s Grubwagon of the Year award, their traditional supporters, lorry drivers, have been joined by professional men – lawyers and even the head chef from a local hotel. Their appearance on *Food and Drink*, says Mick, 'made us respectable. And as far as takings are concerned, it turned our winter into summer.'

Mick and Peg are discriminating eaters themselves. Their prize from the *Sun* was two nights in a London hotel. Peg bursts into a fit of giggles at the memory. 'The carrots were that hard I couldn't get my knife in,' says Mick. And the prices? £7.25 for breakfast! 'Bear in mind,' added Mick, looking round his Lilliputian kitchen and anxious to be fair, 'the surroundings were different, weren't they?'

It's a long day in the lay-by at Kettlesing. Up at 5.30 am, on site by 7 and hard at it until 3.30 pm, with the clearing up still to do; yet Mick and Peg clearly love the life. 'It's seeing the lads satisfied,' says Peg. 'I treat them all as my family.' And why, unlike many of their competitors, do they insist on proper home-cooking when it would be so much easier to heat pre-prepared food? 'I couldn't serve beefburgers all day,' says Peg; 'I'd be bored stiff. The more I cook, the more I experiment.' 'You can go anywhere for hot dogs,' adds Mick; 'but you can't get what Peg's doing now. It's a decent way to make a living.'

With a little culinary arm-twisting, I have persuaded Peg to give us some of her regulars' favourite recipes.

PEG'S BEEF AND BEETROOT PIE
Serves 4

1 lb (450 g) minced meat, cooked
10 oz (275 g) cooked beetroot, diced
1 small onion, diced
1 level teaspoon salt
black pepper
½ teaspoon mixed herbs
1 beef stock cube
2 level tablespoons cornflour

For the suet topping:
4 oz (100 g) self-raising flour
½ teaspoon salt
2 oz (50 g) suet
1 oz (25 g) cheddar cheese, grated
1 egg

Set the oven to 400°F (200°C), gas mark 6. In a bowl, mix the minced beef, beetroot, onion, salt, pepper, mixed herbs and stock cube. Stir in ¾ pint (450 ml) boiling water. Blend the cornflour to a smooth paste with a little water. Stir into the mince mixture, then spoon into a 3-pint (1.75-litre) oven dish. Cover and cook above the centre of the oven for 20 minutes or until hot.

To make the suet topping, sift the flour and salt into a bowl, then stir in the suet and the cheese. Make a well in the centre, add the egg and enough water to make a soft dough. Pull off pieces of dough about the size of a walnut and place on top of the meat mixture. Return to the oven and cook uncovered for about 30 minutes, or until golden brown.

PEG'S POTATO AND SAUSAGE PIE
Serves 4 to 6

2 lb (1 kg) potatoes, peeled and sliced
1 egg plus extra for brushing
1 lb (450 g) sausage meat
Salt and pepper
½ teaspoon dry mustard
2 teaspoons sage and onion stuffing
1 large packet frozen shortcrust pastry
1 onion, finely chopped
Small tin chopped tomatoes
2 oz (50 g) cheddar cheese, grated

Set the oven to 375°F (190°C), gas mark 5.

Parboil the potatoes, then drain. Mix the egg into the sausage meat, then add the salt, pepper, dry mustard and sage and onion stuffing. Roll out the pastry and line a 13 × 9 in (33 × 23 cm) tin with two-thirds of it, reserving the other third for the lid. Put in the sausage mixture and the onion, and pour over the tomatoes. Place the potatoes on top and sprinkle with cheese. Cover with the pastry lid, seal well and brush the top with beaten egg. Cook in the oven for about 1 hour.

PEG'S GUINNESS CAKE

16 oz (450 g) self-raising flour
8 oz (225 g) margarine
8 oz (225 g) soft brown sugar
1 teaspoon mixed spice
1 teaspoon grated nutmeg
8 oz (225 g) sultanas
8 oz (225 g) currants
8 oz (225 g) raisins
5 oz (150 g) glazed cherries
4 eggs
6 fl oz (175 ml) Guinness

Set the oven to 325°F (160°C), gas mark 3. Cream the flour and margarine, then add the sugar, mixed spice, nutmeg and dried fruit. Beat in the eggs, then the Guinness. (Do not add any milk.) If the mixture is a little stiff, add more egg or a little more Guinness. Put into a greased cake tin and bake for about 1 hour.

PEG'S CARROT CAKE

Peg does two other versions of carrot cake. This one has an optional butter-icing topping (very fattening but very delicious).

6 oz (175 g) soft margarine
6 oz (175 g) light brown sugar
3 eggs
10 oz (275 g) self-raising flour
2 level teaspoons baking powder
2 ripe bananas, mashed
4 oz (100 g) carrots, peeled and grated
3 oz (75 g) mixed chopped nuts

For the topping (optional):
2 oz (50 g) butter, softened
2 oz (50 g) full fat cream cheese
4 oz (100 g) icing sugar, sieved
A few drops of vanilla essence

Set the oven to 350°F (180°C), gas mark 4. Place all the ingredients in a mixing bowl and beat for about 2 minutes. Pour into a 9 × 9 in (23 × 23 cm) greased baking tin. Bake for about 1 hour, in the middle of the oven, or until firm to the touch. When the cake is cool, mix the topping ingredients until smooth. Ice the cake, roughing up the topping with a fork. Leave to harden before serving.

RECIPES
MICHAEL BARRY

For me, a real meal has to contain soup, and indeed sometimes the soup contains the meal: great for economy, flavour, and filling hungry stomachs. The trio of soups that follow come from different traditional cuisines, but each one is easy to make, tastes rich and substantial, and fills all the holes. For a meal-in-one, serve them with garlic bread. And make lots – people will keep coming back for more!

MINESTRONE
Serves 6
We tend to think of minestrone as a tomato-based vegetable broth. Not so! It *is* a rich broth and *does* contain vegetables, but only those in season. Traditional minestrone may not contain any tomatoes. The only essentials are dried white or pale green beans and some pasta. You can add Parmesan cheese, of course, and serve with plenty of real crusty bread, or garlic bread.

8 oz (225 g) cannellini or haricot beans
2 pints (1.2 litres) beef stock or water
2 medium onions, chopped
8 oz (225 g) celery, trimmed and chopped
8 oz (225 g) carrots, diced
8 oz (225 g) turnips, diced
¼ pint (150 ml) olive oil
2 oz (50 g) vermicelli or other small pasta
A good pinch each of dried oregano, thyme and basil
Salt and pepper
8 oz (225 g) tomatoes, roughly chopped
4 oz (100 g) green cabbage, shredded
4-8 oz (100-225 g) mushrooms, chopped
Grated Parmesan cheese

Soak the beans overnight. Drain and add to the stock or water. Boil for at least 20 minutes, then simmer for about 2 hours. Sauté the onions, celery, carrots and turnips in the olive oil for 3 to 4 minutes, until softened. Add these and the vermicelli to the beans, season with the herbs, salt and pepper, and simmer until tender. Add the tomatoes, cabbage and mushrooms (adding more water if necessary), and simmer for a further 5 minutes. Serve sprinkled with freshly grated Parmesan cheese.

CORN CHOWDER

Serves 4

Corn, or sweetcorn, is from the New World, as is this soup. The name chowder is supposed to be a corruption of the French word 'chaudron' or cauldron, taken to the Americas by early settlers and used to cook huge, hearty one-pot boil-ups. Modern chowders owe a lot to that tradition, although they are a little more refined than their ancestors. This vegetarian version is as authentic as its more famous fishy relations, the cod and clam chowders.

1 lb (450 g) potatoes, diced
10 oz (275 g) Spanish onions, diced
1 tablespoon vegetable oil
Salt and pepper
½ pint (300 ml) milk
Bay leaf
A pinch of thyme
A pinch of oregano
12 oz (350 g) frozen sweetcorn and peppers, defrosted (or you can use frozen or tinned sweetcorn and add ½ each chopped green and red pepper)

To garnish:
Water biscuits
Fresh parsley, chopped

Gently sweat the diced potatoes and onions in a pan with the oil, over a low heat for about 5 minutes, without browning them. Add a good pinch of salt and pepper, milk, 1 pint (600 ml) water and the herbs. Bring to the boil and simmer for 10 to 15 minutes until the potatoes are soft. Add the sweetcorn and peppers and heat through for another 3 to 4 minutes. Serve with the chopped parsley and crumbled water biscuits over the top.

GOULASH SOUP
Serves 4

I'm not sure whether this is a Hungarian or Austrian dish. The question is in some ways academic because for hundreds of years the Austro-Hungarian Empire was one political entity, and the food travelled with the administrators, just as it did between India and Britain. I suspect that the stew version of this is the Hungarian original, and the lighter soup is a Viennese refinement. Either way, it's one of the most welcoming dishes I know on a chilly evening. I have a vivid memory of consuming a bowl in Innsbruck on an autumn night after a grim crossing of the Alps that still warms me more than a quarter of a century later. Subsequent experience shows it works in the comfort of your own home too!

1 lb (450 g) minced beef
1 tablespoon oil
8 oz (225 g) finely chopped onion
3 tablespoons tomato purée
1 tablespoon paprika powder
1 teaspoon caraway seeds
1 lb (450 g) peeled waxy potatoes
4 tablespoons soured cream

Fry the meat in the oil until brown, add the onions and turn until translucent. Add the tomato purée, paprika and caraway seeds and stir to mix. Pour in 1½ pints (900 ml) water and bring to the boil, then lower the heat to simmer. Cut up the potatoes into pieces ½ inch (1 cm) across and add to the soup. Simmer for 20 minutes, and serve with a spoonful of soured cream in each bowl.

GARLIC BREAD

Here is my own special recipe for garlic bread. The addition of lemon and parsley goes a long way to transforming this pungent parcel into a rather more refined experience. It's safer if everyone at the meal eats it – a dissenter can feel pretty isolated. You can prepare it a day in advance and keep it refrigerated until it's time to bake it.

1 French loaf
2 cloves garlic
1 oz (25 g) parsley, finely chopped
2 oz (50 g) butter
Juice of ½ lemon

Preheat the oven to 375°F (190°C), gas mark 5.

Slice the French loaf three-quarters of the way through, at 1½-inch (4-cm) intervals. Crush the garlic and blend with the parsley, butter and lemon juice, either in a food processor, or by hand. Spread the mixture onto the slices in the loaf, wrap loosely in foil, and bake for 20 minutes. Serve hot.

THE 'CHINESE' YORKSHIRE PUDDING

Traditionally, Yorkshire pudding used to be served before the roast beef to take the edge off the keenest appetite and help the meat go further. This version, though, is slightly different. Jane Grigson tells the story, gleaned from the then *Manchester Guardian*, of a Yorkshire pudding competition once held in Leeds which was won by the chef of a local Chinese take-away. A wonderful story, and absolutely true. Here is the winning recipe to prove it. It really is an oven buster, so leave plenty of head room.

4 oz (100 g) plain flour
2 eggs, beaten
Pinch of salt
½ pint (300 ml) milk
2 tablespoons beef juices or oil

Set the oven to 425°F (220°C), gas mark 7. Whisk the flour, eggs, salt and milk, and leave to stand for 20 to 30 minutes. Put a little of the beef juices or oil into patty tins, and heat the tin for 5 minutes until it's hot, then take out. Fill the patty tins half full with the batter, and bake for 15 minutes or until well risen and golden.

ONION GRAVY

This flavoursome gravy always used to be served with the Yorkshire pudding. Make it from some of the beef drippings.

1 onion, peeled and finely chopped
4 tablespoons beef dripping
2 tablespoons plain flour
½ pint (300 ml) vegetable stock or water
1 teaspoon English mustard
Salt and pepper

Fry the onion in the fat until lightly browned. Add the flour and fry gently, stirring, until it takes on a biscuit brown colour. Add the liquid and stir till smooth. Mix in the mustard, taste and season. Simmer for 3 minutes and serve.

BASIC RISOTTO

Serves 4 to 6

Risottos are the Italian answer to pilaus or paellas – rice dishes with added ingredients cooked in. They are meant to be creamy smooth, not dry and fluffy. The secret is to use special Italian risotto rice, known as Arborio, and to add the liquid a portion at a time as the cooking goes on.

8 oz (225 g) Arborio rice
1 tablespoon oil
1 tablespoon butter
16 fl oz (475 ml) beef stock (warmed)
4 oz (100 g) mushrooms, sliced
A pinch of saffron or turmeric

Fry the rice in the oil and butter for 3 to 4 minutes, then add a small amount of the beef stock, with the mushrooms and saffron or turmeric. Keep adding the stock a little at a time, stirring continuously as it is absorbed. Cook for 15 to 20 minutes for an 'al dente' risotto, and up to 35 minutes if you prefer the rice well-cooked. The finished consistency should be very moist and creamy.

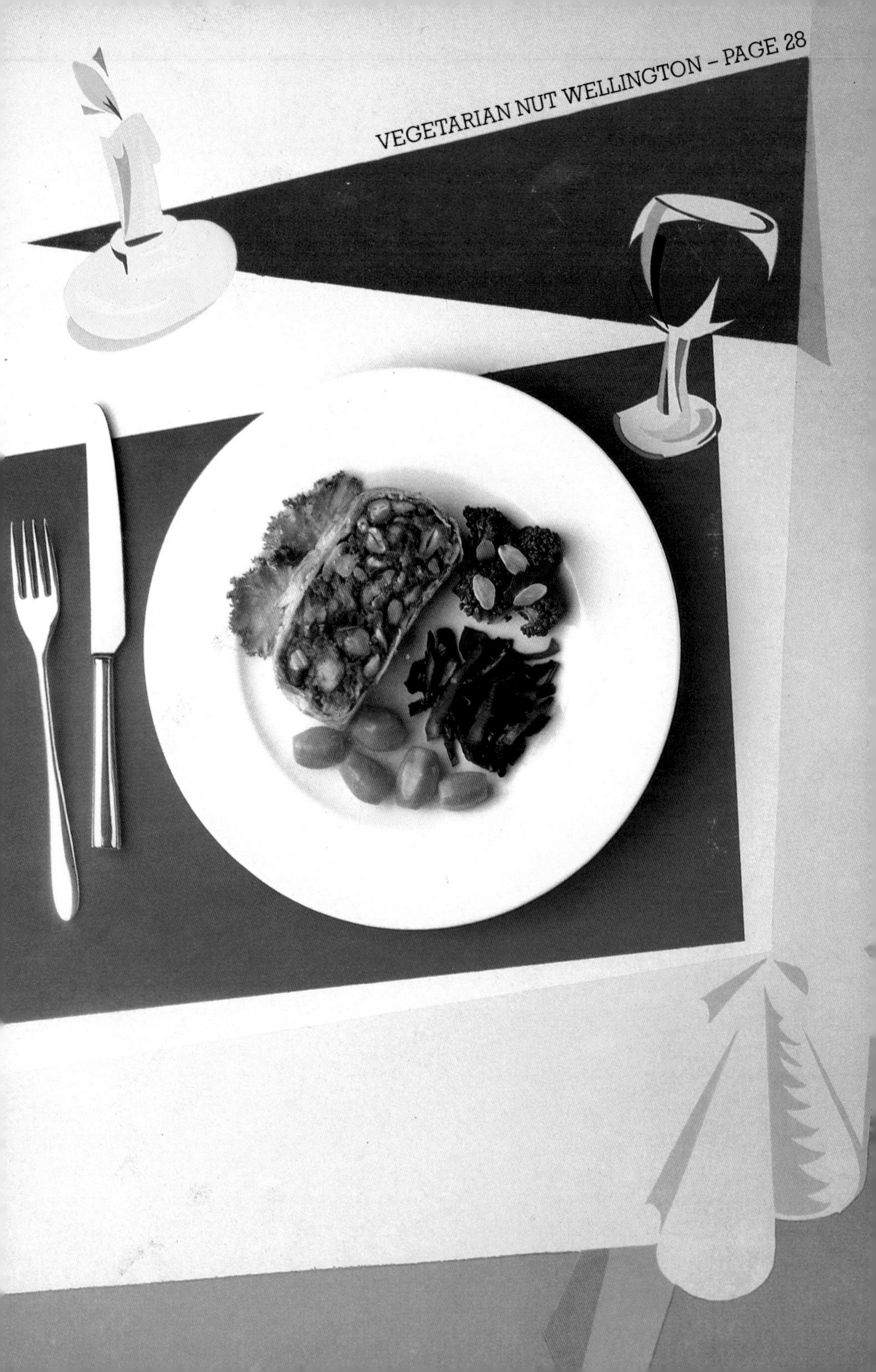
VEGETARIAN NUT WELLINGTON – PAGE 28

HADDOCK MOUSSE – PAGE 46

POTTED SHRIMPS – PAGE 52

STIR-FRY BEEF WITH PEPPERS – PAGE 76

SEAFOOD RISOTTO

Follow the basic recipe but substitute the beef stock with chicken stock or court bouillon, and add:

8 oz (225 g) cleaned squid cut in ¼-in (5-mm) rings
8 oz (225 g) cleaned mussels (see page 48)
4 oz (100 g) shelled prawns
Freshly chopped parsley
1 lemon

Sauté the squid in the oil for 5 minutes, then add the rice, mushrooms and saffron or turmeric. Start adding the stock. Just before the end, add the mussels and prawns, cover, and steam for 5 minutes, or until the mussels open. Adjust the liquid so that the mixture is creamy and smooth, and serve sprinkled with parsley and with a lemon wedge for each serving.

Arborio rice costs 50 to 80 pence per pound, and is available from delicatessens and some supermarkets. It is sometimes labelled 'Italian Risotto Rice'. It has a medium-length grain and is very 'plump' looking. Arborio rice is essential for making risotto. Long grain rice never goes creamy, and short grain, or pudding, rice turns to mush when cooked in this way.

REGIONAL TASTES

INTRODUCTION
CHRIS KELLY

Try asking a Cumbrian what Yarg is, or see if a Londoner can name two speciality foods from Yorkshire, or get a Glaswegian to identify a wine made in Kent. Almost certainly you will be met with blank stares. (Yarg is a delicious Cornish cheese wrapped in nettles, now quite widely available. The Celtic-sounding monosyllable is simply an anagram of the cheesemaker's name – Gray.)

The food industry employs more people in this country than any other industry, we are becoming more and more discriminating about the food we buy and eat, and yet we remain unaware of the rich variety of food and drink, including the finest quality poultry and meat, offered by small producers all over Britain. From the Orkneys to the Scillies, however, there are fast-growing numbers of cottage industries fashioning every imaginable kind of food for our delectation: duck sausages and apple brandy; raised pies and fine vinegar; country wines and home-made jams; smoked fish and pistachio ice-cream; quails, snails and ale. The list is varied and exciting, and the quality excellent.

Small businesses, however, operate on tight budgets and cannot stretch to much advertising, so they remain unknown and unsung to the public at large. There is one group of pioneers in Devon, though, who have fostered a co-operative approach to advertising and marketing with help and encouragement from, among others, Food From Britain (the Government agency created to boost sales of British food and drink at home and abroad), the National Farmers' Union and local councils.

Devon Fare now has more than 70 full producer-members. Under their efficient and delightful whipper-in, Margaret Drake (Marketing Executive), they've chalked up some notable successes. For example, Fourwinds Cruises were so impressed with a Devon Fare presentation that they placed orders with eight of their producers, including one for 23,400 eggs which contained no hormones, additives or colouring, thereby demonstrating a recognition that their passengers prefer fresh, wholesome food with plenty of flavour.

Other counties have been quick to follow Devon's example. In 1987 I had the pleasure of opening Yorkshire Pantry's launch at York Racecourse. Fifty-eight immensely enthusiastic producers were represented, and I managed to sample the delights of every single one. Watching a brewer and his young son, the entire workforce of their minuscule business, proudly describing their traditional methods to the buyer from Macy's of New York was a heart-warming experience.

Yorkshire is a rich county. John Inglis, the energetic organiser of the event, had £40,000 at his disposal. Few other regions have access to that sort of money, nor can they expect big government grants. David Harrison, development manager of Food From Britain's Speciality Foods Programme, says, somewhat ruefully, that 'it runs on a shoestring'. Yet, despite a lack of funds, the flag of enterprise continues to flutter bravely all over Britain: Highland Larder, Galloway Gourmet, Taste of Shropshire, Dorset Harvest, Taste of Norfolk, Wealth of Wiltshire, Herefordshire Hamper and Unicorn (United Cornish Producers) are either up and running or at the development stage; Kent, Warwickshire, Lincolnshire and Cumbria are also contemplating similar ventures. By the time you read this there may well be more names on the list.

In Somerset, *Food and Drink* took part in an extraordinary and dramatic marketing breakthrough. Whether you're pushing your supermarket trolley in Galashiels or Southend, the goods displayed will usually offer few clues as to the local specialities. So how about persuading a leading chain to carry a display of high-quality food and drink from small, local producers?

To their great credit, Gateway immediately accepted the challenge. 'They were marvellous from the word go; completely co-operative,' says Val Evans, Taste of Somerset's tireless Marketing Executive. In February 1988, 14 producers were chosen to represent Taste of Somerset at the Gateway store in Shepton Mallet. On their attractively designed stall were cakes and jams, chutney, cakes, raised game pies, cheese, stuffed breast of duck, wines, bottled spring water, and many more items. Parked nearby was the handsome racing-green bicycle from which Jim Barnard sells his seductive ice-creams (see page 103).

The shop-within-a-shop was open for three days and the response was highly encouraging. Both the takings and the genuine pleasure of the public sent the producers home content, and Gateway's management was also delighted: they were seen to sponsor an obviously worthwhile experiment, which presented their customers with a wider and more intriguing choice than usual. They plan to run the display a second time; this time for a period of three months. If that proves equally successful, they will extend the scheme to ten more stores in the South West.

Today Somerset, tomorrow...? If the idea works in West Country supermarkets, why not nationwide? And if other chains should prove as flexible and supportive as Gateway on this issue, our small regional producers can look forward to a bright future. No longer will their high-quality food and drink be the best-kept secret in Britain's larder.

Shopping around for quality foods

An invaluable new guide, now in its second year – *British Food Finds* – lists thousands of suppliers of regional produce from meats and fish, vegetables and herbs, preserves and sauces, cereals and grains, to confectionery and ice-cream.

Under the heading 'Meat', for example, producers are sub-divided into 'Fresh Meat', 'Bacon and Ham', 'Pâtés and Pastes', 'Pies, Sausages and Smoked Meats'. Under the heading 'Game and Poultry', producers are sub-divided into 'Game Dealers', 'Game Farmers', 'Poultry', 'Pâtés and Pastes', 'Pies', 'Sausages', 'Smoked Food' and 'Eggs'.

The accent is on the traditional and wholesome. Meat is properly hung, where appropriate. Organically reared produce which has legitimately earned one of the symbols of approval is mentioned as such. The pies and sausages tend to be made from traditional ingredients and prepared by traditional methods.

The book is quite expensive, at £14.95, but you do get very comprehensive listings for your money. If unavailable from your local bookshop, you can obtain it from Rich and Green, 1 Moorhouse Road, London W2 5DH, with an additional £2 for postage and packing.

RECIPES
MICHAEL BARRY

Britain's finest quality meat, including game and poultry, is often sold by small regional producers like those mentioned in Chris's introduction. Most of us have a favourite local butcher whose meat we know to be good – if you don't, it's well worth making the effort to find one. Ask your friends, or find out who supplies the better restaurants in your area. You can discover your nearest game dealer by telephoning your local council who issue the necessary licences. Ask for the Environmental Health Office or the Legal Office.

Venison is poised to be the red meat of the future: it's low in fat, contains no additives, and is not factory-farmed. And the price is coming down, too, thanks to the development of commercial herds. The problem with venison, however, is that people often don't know how to cook it. It should be cooked like the drier cuts of beef, and these two recipes, one from Germany and one from the home of the red deer, Scotland, show you how.

VENISON COLLOPS
Serves 4

Collops is the Scottish name for what the French (and the foodies) call *noisettes*: the meat from the eye of a chop. In this recipe, meat rounds cut from the loin or leg will do very well. Use a meat hammer to loosen the fibres and flatten the meat, as you would with a beef steak, as it is cooked quickly. North of the Border, rowanberry jelly is traditionally served with game: its bitter-sweet taste is a perfect complement to the vigorous flavours of game. You can use redcurrant, gooseberry or quince jelly, especially if they aren't too sweet.

1 tablespoon oil
8 collops, or slices of venison cut across the grain
1 oz (25 g) butter
4 tablespoons rowan, redcurrant, gooseberry or quince jelly
1 tablespoon Dijon mustard
5 fl oz (150 ml) single cream
Salt and pepper

Heat a large frying pan, until it is searing hot. Add the oil, then the venison pieces in a single layer. Let them seal for one minute, then turn. Add the butter, turn the heat down and cook for 5 minutes more. Add the jelly and let it melt before adding the mustard and cream. Season the collops, then transfer to plates or a serving dish. Stir the sauce well and pour over the meat. Mashed potatoes and green or red cabbage are good accompaniments.

ROAST VENISON WITH GINGER SAUCE
Serves 6 to 8
The ingredients in this dish may seem a little outlandish, but the combination of the sweet and sour flavours is ideal with a rich-tasting meat like venison. In Germany, the original dish from which the idea came is called *Sauerbraten* and is usually made with a roll of beef like topside, so you can use that instead if you prefer.

> 5 lb (2.25 kg) loin of venison, boned and rolled
> or a rolled topside
> 1 bay leaf
> 1 onion, sliced
> 1 clove garlic, crushed
> ½ pint (300 ml) lager
> 4 tablespoons wine or cider vinegar
> 1 tablespoon brown sugar
> 6 juniper berries
> 6 allspice berries
> 6 peppercorns
> Oil for frying
> 4-5 gingernut biscuits, crushed

Put the meat into a roasting pan. Make the marinade by putting the bay leaf, sliced onion, garlic, lager and vinegar into a saucepan with the brown sugar and bring to the boil. Meanwhile, crush the juniper and allspice berries and the peppercorns with a pestle and mortar. Put these into the hot marinade, stir, and pour over the meat while hot. Leave the meat to marinate for a day or two in a cool place, turning occasionally.

Pre-heat the oven to 350°F (180°C), gas mark 4. Take the meat out of the pan, strain the marinade and reserve. Sauté the joint in a little oil in a large frying pan until browned all over, then place it back in the roasting pan. Pour over the strained marinade, cover the pan with foil, and roast for 20 minutes per lb.

When cooked, transfer the meat to a large serving plate to carve it. Transfer the roasting juices to a saucepan, bring to the boil, adding a little water if necessary, and add the crushed biscuits. They instantly thicken the liquid, making a rich, glossy sauce. Pour this over the carved meat. Serve with red cabbage and boiled potatoes.

BEEF SLICES

The following three recipes are the result of a *Food and Drink* challenge. The plan was to show how delicious meals can result from buying what's available in the shops, rather than setting off with a preconceived shopping list, regardless of what is seasonal or cheap. With a shopping basket full of available ingredients, would it be possible to produce a range of suitable recipes? The answer was a triumphant YES!

All three recipes use the thinly cut beef slices that are now widely available in supermarkets, spring onions and sweet peppers. But the dishes – from places as far apart as Canton and Carlisle – are as different as can be. (If you can't get hold of beef slices, then you can slice a piece of lean steak into suitable slices yourself.)

STIR-FRY BEEF WITH PEPPERS
Serves 4

4 thin slices of lean beef
½ green pepper
½ red pepper
½ yellow pepper
3 spring onions
2 tablespoons vegetable oil
1 dessertspoonful cornflour
1 tablespoon soy sauce

Chop the beef and the vegetables into small strips of equal size about ½ in (1 cm) across. In a wok or frying pan, heat the oil and add the vegetables. Stir-fry for not more than 1½ minutes, remove from the wok and keep warm. Fry the beef until just browned. Mix the cornflour and soy sauce with ½ cup water and add to the wok. Stir until the mixture begins to thicken, then add the vegetables. Stir all the ingredients, then serve immediately with rice.

PAUPIETTES DE BOEUF MOUTARDINES
Serves 4

1 tablespoon olive oil
1 oz (25 g) butter
4 thin slices of lean beef
8 fl oz (250 ml) sour cream
½ red pepper, chopped
½ green pepper, chopped
½ yellow pepper, chopped
1 teaspoon grainy mustard
10 fresh, tinned or bottled green peppercorns
Salt

Heat the olive oil in a frying pan, then add the butter. When the butter has just stopped foaming, add the beef. Brown on both sides, then cook for 4 minutes, or slightly longer if you like it well done. Add the sour cream, stir and add the chopped peppers. Cook for a further 2 to 3 minutes before adding the mustard, peppercorns and salt to taste. Stir again and serve.

BEEF OLIVES
Serves 8

4 oz (100 g) fresh, soft breadcrumbs
1 egg
1 large pinch thyme
1 large pinch marjoram
Salt and pepper
1 small red pepper, finely chopped
1 small green pepper, finely chopped
2 spring onions, finely chopped
A little milk
8 thin slices of lean beef
A little oil
A little tomato purée

Mix the breadcrumbs with the beaten egg, herbs and seasoning, and add the vegetables. Mix well, adding a little milk if necessary. Place a small spoonful of the mixture on each slice of beef, and roll up. Secure each 'olive' with a wooden cocktail stick, and fry in the oil until just browned. Remove from the heat. Add 3 fl oz (85 ml) water and the tomato purée and return to the heat to simmer for 20 minutes. Don't forget to remove the cocktail sticks – they are *very* crunchy!

LOTS OF LAMB

As a result of increased interest in healthy eating, most butchers and supermarkets now sell new lamb cuts, such as 'leg steaks'. These have a lot less fat than traditional cuts. Butchers are also more willing to trim the excess fat off other cuts such as loin chops.

GRILLED LAMB LEG STEAKS

You can buy these with or without the bone. The dish gets its character from the strongly aromatic Mediterranean herbs; you can leave the lavender out, but it's a pity, as it gives a gentle, unique hint of hot, sun-baked hillsides.

For each leg steak you need:

A little olive oil
A pinch each of lavender, rosemary, oregano, and thyme
1 teaspoon quince or redcurrant jelly
Salt and pepper

Pre-heat the grill to high. Trim any fat from the steaks, and brush one side with the oil. Sprinkle over a pinch of each herb. Grill for 3 to 5 minutes. Turn over, lightly coat with jelly and grill for another 3 to 5 minutes. Season and serve.

LAMB CHOPS MILANESE

Serves 2 to 3

Lamb is not a meat much associated with Italy, but this dish is definitely worth mentioning. While hardly a low-fat recipe, it does have that very Italian virtue of spreading a small amount of meat a long way. It's also ideally suited to the thin, machine-cut chops on sale in many butchers at low prices.

1 egg
1 lb (450 g) lamb chops, thin cut
2 cups fresh white breadcrumbs
Grated rind of ½ lemon (optional)
4 tablespoons olive oil
1 tablespoon butter

Beat the egg and dip the chops in it, one at a time. Put the breadcrumbs with the grated lemon rind, if used, in a deep bowl. Place the chops in it and turn until well coated with the crumbs. Heat the oil in a large frying pan and fry the chops gently, in a single layer, for 6 minutes each side. Drain the oil, add the butter and turn up the heat until the sizzling stops. Serve with a green salad and sauté potatoes (if you dare!).

TANDOORI LAMB CHOPS
Serves 3 to 4

Tandoori-cooked dishes, or spiced marinated food baked in a dry oven, are now very common in our Indian restaurants, yet the technique only emerged a few years ago from its Punjabi homeland. There, they are far more adventurous about what to marinate and bake, and chops are a standard item.

Though you can make your own tandoori 'mix', it's hardly worth the trouble. Buy one with a good 'name', use only half the quantity recommended, and the result will be fine.

5 fl oz (150 ml) yoghurt
1 tablespoon tandoori mix
1 tablespoon lemon juice
1 garlic clove, crushed
1½ lb (750 g) lamb chops

Combine the yoghurt, tandoori mix, lemon juice and garlic. Marinate the chops in the mixture for at least 4 hours, preferably overnight, refrigerated. Heat the oven to 425°F (220°C), gas mark 7 and bake the chops for 13 to 15 minutes. Pour off the fat, and serve with fresh yoghurt, chutney and warm pitta bread, or Indian breads if you prefer.

CAWL
Serves 4

Cawl is Wales's answer to the *pot-au-feu*, a two-course meal cooked in one pot. Customarily, cawl was made from scrag end or neck of lamb, but for a special occasion a trimmed, boned and rolled shoulder is ideal.

2 lb (1 kg) leeks
2½ lb (1.25 kg) lamb shoulder, boned and rolled
or 3 lb (1.5 kg) neck of lamb, cut in chops
and trimmed of fat
1 celery stalk
1 sprig fresh thyme
2 bay leaves
8 oz (225 g) swede
8 oz (225 g) parsnips
Boiled potatoes and chopped parsley to serve

Trim and wash the leeks, and tie half in a bundle with a piece of string that can be hung over the side of a casserole dish. Cut the celery in half, put the thyme and bay leaves in the hollow of one half, cover with the other half, and tie together with string. Cut the root vegetables into thick pieces, and put all the ingredients, apart from the remaining leeks, into a large casserole dish, and cover with water. Simmer for 25 minutes per lb of lamb. At the end of the cooking time, take the bundle of leeks out, chop the reserved leeks, and add to the casserole. Simmer for a further 10 to 15 minutes.

To serve the first course, fill soup bowls with the broth from the casserole, adding a pinch of chopped parsley. For the second course, arrange the meat in the centre of a large serving plate, and surround with the vegetables. Serve with potatoes boiled in their skins.

PEKING DUCK
Serves 4

It's quite easy to find Peking roast duck in this country, served with pancakes and the traditional savoury plum and hoisin sauces. But in China the same duck would be used to make two further courses. If you do as they do and just add some rice and a few vegetables, you will have three courses for four people from one bird.

4½–6 lb (2–2.75 kg) duck
1 tablespoon brown sugar
1 cucumber
4 spring onions
12 mini-pancakes (see below)
6 tablespoons either hoisin sauce or Chinese plum sauce
(or plum jam mixed with 1 tablespoon soy sauce)

Discard any visible fatty pieces, then place the duck in a large casserole and pour over a kettle of boiling water. Drain and leave to dry for at least 4 hours, or overnight, but not in the refrigerator. This will crisp the skin when it roasts.

Pre-heat the oven to 400°F (200°C), gas mark 6. Put the duck on a wire rack over a roasting tin, and roast for 40 minutes. Dissolve the brown sugar in 1 tablespoon of water and brush over the duck, breast side up, and roast for another 40 minutes. Remove from the oven and leave to rest for 10 minutes.

Cut the cucumber and spring onions into very thin slivers. Heat the pancakes in the oven for 5 minutes. Skin the duck and cut the crispy skin into small pieces. Brush each pancake with your choice of sauce. Put a few slivers of cucumber and spring onion on top, cover with the crispy duck skin, and roll up the pancakes by folding in each side and turning up the bottom to stop the filling falling out.

CHINESE PANCAKES
Makes 12

8 oz (225 g) plain flour
Large pinch of salt
A little sesame or vegetable oil

Sift the flour and salt into a mixing bowl, add 4 fl oz (120 ml) water and mix until they form a dough. Knead lightly on a floured surface and divide into 12 equal pieces. Roll out into circles the size of tea plates. Lightly brush the surface of 6 circles with the oil on one side. Cover each one carefully with another circle and roll out gently.

Fry the pancakes in a dry frying pan or griddle for 3 to 4 minutes, turning once, until firm, but not too brown. Cool for a few minutes then peel the pancakes apart. These pancakes can be made in advance and stored in an airtight container until needed.

STIR-FRIED DUCK

This is made with the flesh from the same duck you have just eaten the skin of. In addition you will need:

1 tablespoon oil
1 garlic clove, crushed
Pinch of ginger
8 oz (225 g) beansprouts
½ red pepper, cut into thin strips
½ green pepper, cut into thin strips
1 tablespoon soy sauce

Pull the duck meat from the bone and slice thinly. Heat the oil in a wok or large frying pan with the crushed garlic and ginger. Add the duck and vegetables, and stir-fry for about 3 minutes. Add the soy sauce, stir and serve with plain boiled rice.

DUCK SOUP
The third dish from the duck!

Duck carcass
1 teaspoon salt
½ Chinese leaf cabbage

Put the duck carcass in a saucepan with water to cover, add the salt and bring to the boil. Simmer for 20 to 30 minutes. Cut the cabbage into bite-size pieces and add to the soup. Simmer for a further 5 minutes. Serve without the bones, after the rich duck dishes, as a palate cleanser.

Knife sharpening
For all meat and poultry preparation, a sharp knife is essential. There are an increasing number of knife-sharpening gadgets on the market, but the old-fashioned technique of sharpening with a steel is still the best. Follow these steps and you can't go wrong.

1 Grasp the handle of the steel firmly and place the tip securely on a flat surface.
2 Hold the steel vertically in one hand and the knife in the other at 20 degrees to the steel.
3 Slide the blade of the knife down the steel, drawing it from tip to handle as though 'carving' the steel.
4 Ensure that the blade is inclined no more than 20 degrees away from the steel, or you will blunt rather than sharpen the knife.

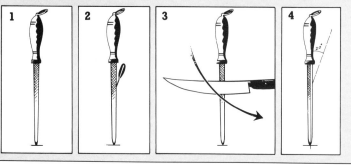

CHRISTMAS HINTS
For a perfectly carved turkey this year, follow the technique demonstrated by David Gay, sous-chef at the Waldorf Hotel and 1987 Master Carver of Britain, on our Christmas Show.

1 Before the turkey is cooked remove the wishbone, situated at the head (the opposite end to the 'parson's nose'). Use a very sharp knife to cut away the flesh around the wishbone so that you can grasp it. Twist it sharply and it will come away.

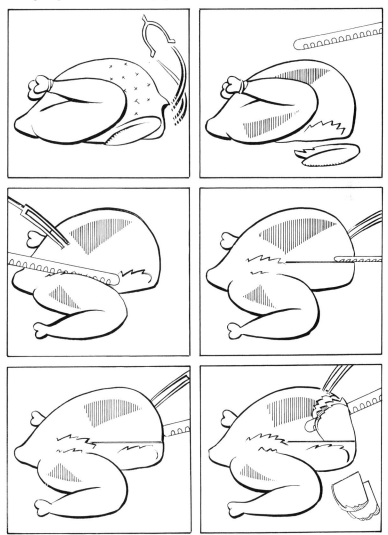

2 Roast the turkey according to your chosen method for the required length of time. Remove from the oven and let it stand for a few minutes.

3 With a sharpened carving knife, remove the wing and leg on one side of the bird. Then, cutting vertically on that side, separate the breast meat from the breast bone without entirely removing it; and cutting horizontally, separate the breast from the base of the bird in the same way.

4   Then carve the breast portion you have separated, diagonally to the bird. As you reach the breast bone you should then gradually straighten the angle of carving to allow access to the remaining breast meat. This technique gives even slices which can be arranged neatly on a plate. It also yields a greater number of slices. Repeat the process on the second breast.

5   Carve the brown meat off the legs and wings.

APRICOT AND PEAR STUFFING FOR A CHRISTMAS GOOSE

More and more people are choosing geese for Christmas. Here's my favourite stuffing, and don't forget to accompany it with traditional apple sauce. The acidity of the fruit will balance the richness of the bird.

4 oz (100 g) dried apricots
4 oz (100 g) dried pears
6 oz (175 g) breadcrumbs
1 bunch spring onions, chopped
2 tablespoons parsley, chopped
1 pinch of fresh or dried sage
2 eggs
Grated rind and juice of 1 lemon

Soak the apricots and pears overnight. Chop them well and mix together with all the other ingredients, and stuff the bird. Weigh after stuffing to calculate the cooking time: 25 minutes per lb.

Turkeys can be perked up with a change of stuffing. Instead of the usual sausage-meat stuffing, try a cup each of lightly cooked cranberries, sweet corn and breadcrumbs bound with an egg, or a handful of chopped parsley mixed with 2 cups of soft fresh breadcrumbs, a chopped sautéed onion, the grated rind and juice of a lemon, a teaspoon each of thyme and marjoram and 4 oz (100 g) of butter.

BEEF OLIVES – PAGE 77

PEKING DUCK WITH CHINESE PANCAKES – PAGE 80

BLACKBERRY COBBLER – PAGE 109

HOME·MADE ICE·CREAM – PAGE 111

Jill Goolden's hints for choosing wines to accompany poultry and meat

By following the sweetness code for white wines (from 1 to 9) and the code for red wines based on fullness of body and strength of flavour (from A to E), now widely displayed on bottles, wine can be bought more discerningly.

Turkey
Can take red or white, but at Christmas the chances are you will want a special wine such as a white Alsace Riesling (2), Alsace Pinot Blanc (3), a red Beaujolais Nouveau (A), or the better quality Beaujolais Villages (B). For a particular treat, try a more expensive Beaujolais, named after a specific village such as Fleurie or Julienas (B).

Goose and Duck
You could choose a beefy red such as Châteauneuf du Pape or an Australian Shiraz (D,E) to match a goose's strong, gamey flesh. But be careful – they could overpower the meat. As an alternative, for both goose and duck, I recommend an Australian Chardonnay (2) or an Alsace Gewürztraminer (3) – both whites. For a red, how about a claret (Bordeaux) (C)?

Chicken
Can take red or white. Choose a light-bodied red (A,B or possibly C) and a white on the dry side of medium (1–4).

Beef and Lamb
There is a lot of sense in following the old rule of red for both these meats, as they tend to overpower white. Basically you want to match weight with weight – a heavy dish calls for a fuller-bodied wine – and strength of flavour with strength of flavour: delicate dishes call for light, delicate wines, powerfully spicy dishes for big heavyweights. Follow the A–E code here.

Venison
Châteauneuf du Pape or Hermitage – both strong reds from the Rhône (D/E) – or Australian Shiraz (E). These wines are made from the same grape variety and have the body to cope with strongly flavoured game.

ENJOYING WINES

WINE-TASTING
JILL GOOLDEN

Cartoons and caricatures can be cruel. In a couple of strokes, the pen slashes straight to the point – and you wonder why you didn't instantly see the victim in that light yourself. Recently, I discovered that impersonations can be cruel too, or at least a bit uncomfortable in their accuracy. I was minding my own business on a sunny afternoon, when into my sights came a gangly teenager. And what was she doing? It was immediately apparent that she was 'doing' me wine-tasting. She was like a perpetual-motion ostrich, rocking backwards and forwards over a bowl of water, when suddenly, mid-sentence, her nose took a dive into a make-believe glass, the 'glass' moving simultaneously up to meet her conk. In an instant I recognised an action that has become second nature to me, an integral part of my everyday life.

I never give a thought to the mechanics of wine-tasting. Like learning to change gear on a car, once you've mastered it, you never give it another thought. The peering, swirling, sniffing, slurping, gargling and spitting business of wine-tasting is merely gear-changing, as it were: the means to the end, and that end is being able better to appreciate the wine. All the ritual associated with examining wine in such detail is necessary when tasting wine seriously, as opposed to socially. It is done to learn as much as possible about the wine so that you can judge its quality, and how well made it is; whether it's worth the money; or (as in the *Food and Drink* Quiz) to identify the wine: the variety of grape from which it is made, the sort of climate it grew up in, how young or old it is and any other details. The technique is worth mastering, although to begin with, you'll feel a bit of a nut going through all the contortions. You'll find, however, that they do work, and in my step-by-step guide, I'll explain how and why.

You need a glass with a stem and a bowl that curves in at the top. The ordinary Paris goblet – the shape you find most often in pubs and cheap-and-cheerful restaurants – is fine, or you can use the tulip design. The reason for this is described in steps 1, 2 and 3.

Step 1 Fill the glass about a third full, no more, and never higher than the widest part of the Paris goblet. Always handle the glass by the stem, so you don't heat chilled white wine with the warmth of your hand on the glass, or further warm a red wine at room temperature. Keeping your sticky mitts off the bowl of the glass also ensures that it remains clear and doesn't distort the colour of the wine. When tasting a number of wines, you can use the same glass for each wine, as long as you don't warm it up or dirty the sides.

Step 2 Look at the colour of the wine, by holding it up against a white background. To see it in more detail, tilt the glass and look down into the wine lying in the curve of the bowl against a white tablecloth or piece of paper. Red wines change from purply red, when young, to a little rusty, with a darker rim when more mature. White wines can be almost as colourless as water or take on the hue of old gold in an older wine, so the colour helps you judge its age and 'body'. Generally, for both red and white wines, the lighter-bodied wines are paler and the fuller-bodied are darker in colour.

Step 3 Holding the glass by the stem, swirl the wine round in the bowl, disrupting the surface. This is quite an art, and can be fairly hazardous when you first try. To play safe, keep the base of the glass on the table while you swirl, or just jiggle the glass enough to break the wine's surface. This releases the aromas into the bowl of the glass, where they are trapped by the narrowing of the glass towards the rim. You fill the glass only a third full to leave plenty of room for the wine to ripple, for the released aromas to collect and, of course, for your nose!

Immediately after your brief swirl, get your nose right down into the glass and breathe in deeply, giving a good sniff. Your sense of smell, although acute once trained, is only short-lived, so after a few deep sniffs, lower the glass and clear your nostrils with some deep breaths, before starting again.

Step 4 Now for the first taste. Your taste-buds are distributed all over the surface of your tongue, different areas of the tongue picking up different types of taste. There are only four essential tastes, of which three are relevant in wine-tasting: sweetness, which is picked up on the tip of the tongue; acidity, which is picked up on the upper edges, and bitterness, which is sensed at the back. Make sure all parts of your tongue come into contact with the wine. Your sense of smell is more powerful than your sense of taste and can be used as a 'booster' while you taste the wine. The trick is to breathe in air while tasting the wine, and coating all your buds.

Take a good-sized sip and first 'chew' the liquid round in your mouth, but don't swallow! While the mouthful of wine is still being held on top of your tongue, open your lips as though about to whistle, and suck in little gusts of air, which should pass over the wine, carrying the bouquet, or aroma, to the back of your throat, where your sense of smell can pick it up. (Be careful experimenting with this technique at first, since if you catch the wine with the air, you can choke!) If you were going on to taste lots of wines after this mouthful, and wanted to keep your wits about you, this would be the time to spit the wine out. If not, then swallow.

Step 5 It is entirely possible, especially after practice, to taste a wine thoroughly and completely without swallowing it. This may appear to destroy all the fun, but is necessary if you are planning to study a number of wines. The spitting-out bit is another marvellous subject for the impersonator, since it isn't actually a normal part of everyday life, but it is useful to know how to do it if you ever go to an official wine-tasting. The key thing, when spitting out a mouthful of wine, is to be positive. You have actually to spit, and curiously, the more force you put behind it, the tidier and more accurate you are. A good place to practise in private is the bathroom. With water, not wine.

So here you have the technique. Recording what you actually discover during all these contortions is the next step. There is a whole language of specialised terms used by wine-tasters and wine snobs, but you certainly don't have to go on a language course to be able to appreciate and judge a wine. You will very soon develop your own reference points, and 'know what you mean' by your own choice of language.

Essentially the things you are looking for are:

BOUQUET

Does this wine have a powerful aroma, a delicate aroma, virtually no smell at all? Is the 'bouquet' pleasant? Fruity? Flowery? Earthy? Vegetably? Smoky? Chemical? Does it remind you of another scent? The red Cabernet Sauvignon grape, for instance, can smell powerfully of blackcurrants, and the white Sauvignon grape of gooseberries.

TASTE

When you first taste the wine, does it seem 'fruity'? It is, after all, made from fruit, but does this show? Is the taste clean from start to finish, or are there some other 'off flavours' creeping in? Has it got a fresh nip of acidity; too much acidity, which makes it rather sharp, or too little, which makes it 'soupy' and bland? In a red wine, can you taste the slightly bitter tannin? Tannin, present in the skin and stalks of the grapes, gives body to and helps preserve red wines intended to mature for a few years. By the time you taste the wine, the tannin, which gives a drying sensation on the sides of your tongue, ideally should have mellowed and married in with the other flavours. It shouldn't dominate the fruit. Are all the flavours in harmony with each other, giving a balanced whole? Champagne, for instance, is generally a blend of many different wines made from different grapes and in some Champagnes, the components are not all married in to give a perfect whole. One element or other may dominate, which is, of course, undesirable.

Above all, do you like it? Is it worth the money? Will you buy it again?

Corkscrews

Corkscrews come in all shapes and sizes, but no one has yet bettered the basic design of the open helix. If the shaft is solid, it is liable to break the cork and the displaced particles will be forced down to the bottom until they fall into the wine. The key test of a good open-helix corkscrew is whether you can drop a matchstick down its centre.

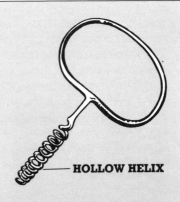

HOLLOW HELIX

One of the most efficient corkscrews available is the Screwpull which incorporates the open helix, with a non-stick coating, into an ingenious no-effort design.

Screwpull have recently rationalised their range. The following two models are now available in all good kitchen shops and department stores:

Pocket Spinhandle £9.95
Screwpull £9.95

Pocket Spinhandle comes with a small blade, for removing foil. Alternatively, Screwpull also make a separate gadget for this purpose:

Foil Cutter £4.95

WINE CONTAINERS

For centuries, wines came in only one container, the bottle, recently standardised in size at 75 cls, which is three-quarters of a litre. But such a size doesn't necessarily give you the precise amount you want. Say two of you just want a glass each, or even two glasses each; that leaves you with opened unconsumed wine which it would be heresy to throw away. You could buy half-bottles, if there were more around, but few people sell them, and there's a pitifully narrow choice. Once exposed to the air, wine does begin to go off, so what do you do?

After much brow-furrowing the whizz-kids in the wine business came up with some suggestions to help you enjoy a single glass of wine. They introduced the wine box which contains a sealed bag of wine accessible via a tap with a valve which excludes the air. Though fine in theory, they are expensive to buy (you have to get at least 3 litres at a time), occasionally inefficient in operation (the wine does, after a while, deteriorate) and generally contain uninteresting wines.

Another idea was for double-serve cans, but these are again expensive and contain uninspiring wines. Then there was a spate of wines in mini-cardboard boxes, like individual fruit juices, which didn't prove popular. So it was back to the good old bottle, and the original problem of how to preserve what is left after you have had as much as you want.

Now, at last, the whizz-kids have cracked it. There are two efficient methods of preserving the wine left in an opened bottle. Both work – I use them a lot and have no complaints – and each is ingenious in its simplicity. The first miracle-worker to appear on the scene was the Vacuvin. The mechanism consists of a special bung inserted in the neck of the opened bottle. A small pump – not unlike some types of corkscrew in appearance – fits over it, and, with a few easy strokes, you draw the air out of the bottle, leaving only the wine and a vacuum inside.

We put this gadget through its paces at the South Bank Polytechnic, where it was observed over the period of a week. The conclusion was that it gave a partial, but reasonably effective, vacuum. Over comparatively short periods (10 days, say) that is adequate, and although the wine isn't absolutely perfect second time around, it is certainly pleasant enough to drink – it would take an expert to spot the difference.

Watching the programme at home in Northwich, Cheshire, Harold Tarrant, who had quite obviously been concealing his talent for invention for all his eighty years, suddenly had a brainwave. If keeping the air off the wine is all that is required, he thought, I can do better than that. And so he went out to his kitchen, found a foodbag, and perfected the Tarrant method of wine preservation. First poke a clean foodbag into the neck of a bottle, using the wrong end of a knitting needle, then either fill it with water, making sure all air is excluded, or with air which you blow into the bag through a straw. Getting the bag out again before pouring the wine is another art, achieved again with a needle, this time poked down outside the bag inside the neck of the bottle so a vacuum isn't formed.

Harry demonstrated his method with supreme accomplishment for us on air, but when I got home from the studio that night, I found that my husband, Paul, had had a go. With demonstrably less skill than Harry had shown, he had made a complete dog's dinner out of a half-full bottle of Minervois, using a red bin liner which burst. My advice is – always use a foodbag and make sure it's a strong one. (And, if you are as impractical as Paul, further advice – don't attempt it!)

Another viewer, Dr John Moillet (from Worcester), also let us in on his secret wine-preserving method, which simply involves adding two crushed 50 mg vitamin C tablets to the wine before recorking or covering the opening of the bottle. Rather warily I tried this adventurous method on a bottle of good Muscadet, and extraordinarily, the ascorbic acid (vitamin C) not only kept the wine in good nick, it actually improved it.

While *Food and Drink* viewers were busily perfecting their own wine-preserving methods at home, the Wine Society, our longest-established wine club at 150 years old, was busily carrying out its own tests on another new device, the Wine Preserver. The results suggested that over longer periods, it probably works better than the Vacuvin. The Wine Preserver essentially converts one of the oldest tricks in the wine-making industry for use in the home. Nitrogen has two invaluable features useful for preserving wine; it is inert (so it has no effect on other substances it comes into contact with), and it is heavier than air. If you cover the surface of a wine with a layer of nitrogen, the air is excluded with no damage to the wine. So the Preserver takes the form of a canister of nitrogen which you aim into an open bottle with a long straw. Give a brief squirt, and although you can see absolutely nothing happening, there is now a blanket of nitrogen sitting on top of your wine, keeping it fresh until the next time you want to pour some (quite normally) from the bottle.

Vacuvin costs £6.99 for a pack containing one pump and two stoppers (further stoppers, £1.75 for two) from Victoria Wine, John Lewis, Majestic Wine Warehouse, House of Fraser.

The Wine Preserver is available from:
ROTOKEG Products Ltd.,
Unit 7,
Allen Road,
Rushden,
Northants NN10 0DU

Send a cheque or postal order made payable to ROTOKEG, for £4.95 (which includes postage and packing).

LAYING DOWN WINES

I never cease to marvel at the many wonders of wine; it really is the most surprising drink, and by that I mean capable of springing surprises. And it is perhaps that, above all its other qualities, that puts it into a totally different class from, say, grape juice, Lucozade, gin or even crème de menthe. It can pack into a single glass an infinite range of subtly individual scents and flavours that complement, harmonise and contrast with each other. And in the so-called 'fine' wines – in general the more expensive varieties – this medley constantly changes in the bottle and, once poured, even in the glass.

From the moment the grapes are picked, wine goes through innumerable different changes of flavour. The first ones are fairly obvious; the juice from the crushed grapes quickly transforms from fresh to fermented and the chemical reaction of the yeast on the sugar alters the character almost unrecognisably. The wine then alters every day as it starts to mature, and in most instances, this maturing process continues until the moment the wine is drunk. (The exceptions are the few, mainly very cheap, wines scientifically treated to prevent any further development in the bottle.)

Most wine is generally given time to mature in the cellar where it is made before being bottled; longer for reds than for whites, but anything from a few days to a few years. This may take place in anything from large stainless steel, tower-like vats to small oak barrels. During this time, the harsher elements in the wine – bitterness contributed by the tannin derived, in the case of red wines, from the grapes' stalks and skins – soften, the flavours 'come out', and the bouquet starts to blossom. The business of being made into wine is quite a trauma for the grape juice: it takes time for it to settle and for the component flavours to marry together to give a harmonious, delicious whole.

In the old days, before we intervened in the wine-making process with 'new technology', wines used to take considerably longer to mature fully. Sometimes wine merchants would keep them during their maturing years, but usually the customer would plan ahead and buy wines before they were ready to drink, and store them in a cellar for many years, perhaps even decades. Two important developments have taken place since then. The first is that wines take much less time to be ready to drink. The vast majority are out on the shelves and ready to pour when only a year or two old. The second is that very few of us have cellars any more.

But there are some wines (usually the slightly more special wines), which benefit from being kept. Indeed, apart from the cheapest wines (the lowest quality each country produces, such as vins de table and vino da tavola) and such wines as Beaujolais Nouveau and Asti or Moscato Spumante which are made specifically to be drunk young, a period in the cupboard under the stairs will do wines no harm at all, and could surprise you by doing genuine good.

A while back, I was given a case of inexpensive Champagne. The first bottle I tasted seemed a little green and acidic – a symptom of being too young – and so I put the other eleven under my bed and forgot about them for a year, until I moved house. On arriving at our new house lots of well-wishers dropped by and so, during the first couple of weeks, we polished off most of the remaining bottles. They had improved beyond recognition. Indeed, some of the well-wishers were wine luminaries who puzzled over what Champagne this could be – it was definitely an extremely good vintage of a noble Champagne, they agreed.

Champagne is one of the less obvious wines to benefit from keeping for a while. The usual candidates are reds, and some of the more helpful supermarkets and high street wine shops indicate either on the blurb on the shelf or on the back label which ones will benefit from keeping, or 'laying down'. The classic place to buy wines – usually at advantageous prices, incidentally – before they are ready to drink, is wine merchant shops, where you can rely on helpful sales people to advise you on the best buys, and a much more welcoming atmosphere than you might imagine.

To store wine, you need a draught-free spot, away from direct sunlight (in the dark is best) with an even temperature, preferably on the cool side. I recently had an estimate for insulating a corner of my garage to keep it at a constant temperature and was pleasantly surprised to hear that it could be accomplished for approximately £100. The bottles should always be kept lying down, so that the cork remains moist. If it dries out, air could get in to spoil the wine. At one time, I kept my wine in lengths of clay drainage pipe stacked against a wall. They kept the wine at a splendidly even temperature, and looked attractive, too.

On the rack

A whole range of inexpensive wine racks are available from furniture shops, kitchen shops and specialist home brew shops. Here's an indication of the prices:

Wooden rack which 'concertinas' out to take 16 bottles (from Boots)   £3.95

Wooden blocks and metal strips for self-assembly.
Any size available.
(from home brew shops and David Mellor)
For 16 bottles   £4.50

Steel or pine racks, ready assembled
(from Habitat)
Pine (for 12 bottles)   £5.95
Steel (for 16 bottles)   £5.95

Purpose-made hexagonal honeycomb clay pipes from:
Antrad Designs,
The Sussex Suite,
City Gates,
2–4 Southgate,
Chichester,
Sussex PO19 1DJ
Minimum purchase 6 units (for 30 bottles)   £72.00

Lead foil

Most wine bottles now sold in supermarkets and off-licences have plastic or aluminium foil around the top. The traditional covering, lead foil, tends only to be found on finer wines because it is a much more expensive material. There are exceptions – some quite inexpensive Spanish wines still use lead foil – so heed this recent warning from the Ministry of Agriculture, Fisheries and Food.

After tests in their laboratories, they found that around one-fifth of wines with lead foil tops contained more than the legally permitted amount of lead. This is because wine seeping through the cork, over a period of time, corrodes the foil, forming lead tartrate crystals – a white powder deposited on the neck of the bottle – and the danger is that the crystals can end up in your glass. So the advice with lead foil tops is: WIPE THE NECK OF THE BOTTLE BEFORE YOU POUR.

A damp cloth is all you need.

Wine clubs

Unlike book clubs, wine clubs don't exist to give you bargains, but they do give you excellent choice and good advice. Most importantly, they sell wines of consistent quality guaranteed by the club. As well as regular newsletters, pre-selection if you like, special trips and home delivery, many clubs will also store your wines for you. Three of Britain's leading wine clubs are:

The Wine Club,
New Aquitaine House,
Paddock Road,
Reading,
Berks RG4 0JY
Telephone: (0734) 481711
Standard membership: £5 + £3 per annum. Life membership: £50.

The Wine Mine Club,
Vintner House,
River Way,
Harlow,
Essex CM20 2EA
Telephone: (0279) 416291
Membership: £5 per annum.

The Wine Society,
Gunnels Wood Road,
Stevenage,
Herts SG1 2RG
Telephone: (0438) 314161
Membership: £20 secures a (transferable) lifetime share in the society, which also accrues dividends.

Many local wine merchants also run excellent wine clubs. The choice may be smaller but you do get a very personal service.

SWEET THINGS

INTRODUCTION
CHRIS KELLY

Picture a misty Somerset lane on a spring morning. Rising in the background, like a grass pyramid, is Glastonbury Tor. Suddenly, round a bend in the road, appears a knight puissant on a charger (perhaps the ghost of Lancelot?) bearing a strange device. It's Jim Barnard pedalling his ice-cream cart to Shepton Mallet. Unromantic maybe, but an extraordinary story all the same. Jim was once a forensic scientist. On a trip to the United States he fell for American ice-cream and decided to emulate it here. We'll come back to him a bit later.

Meanwhile, cut to Magdalene Street, Cambridge, 4.00 am Saturday. Hans Schweitzer, the son of a German architect, is arriving for work. With his small team, he'll spend the next twelve hours creating a wide range of utterly irresistible confections, from brioches to hand-made chocolates and wedding cakes. The route that brought him here is just as unexpected as the one taken by Jim Barnard.

Varied though their lives are, both men share common attitudes to food. Neither will settle for anything short of the best; they both insist on high-quality fresh ingredients; and they both love what they do. Their attitude is still the exception rather than the rule in Britain.

As we flash back to Somerset, I have to admit that Jim Barnard was only in the saddle for the sake of our camera. Even after barely eighteen months' trading, his business is going too successfully to allow the boss to spend precious time on a vendor's bicycle. It all started at Scotland Yard. Jim was working at the Metropolitan Police Forensic Science Laboratory but he wasn't happy. 'Rapes and murders didn't frighten me. It was seeing a piece of paper... something about a pension. The Civil Service had a whole career planned for me. They even knew my date of retirement.'

There followed a fateful posting to the United States, where Jim helped establish a Forensic Science teaching course at Northeastern University in Boston. The local supermarket had already introduced him to various brands of ice-cream, but the real conversion happened when he visited Steve's ice-cream parlour, not far from Harvard in a not particularly smart part of town. Although it was winter, he was surprised to find a queue stretching round the block. The moment he tasted Steve's formula, Jim understood why. 'It was a revelation to me. To someone brought up on synthetic ice-cream, it was a different world.' In fact, Jim was soon so hooked that he went on a lunchtime diet of carrots and crispbread so he could do justice to Steve's cold comfort in the evening.

On his return to Britain, rather than take up where he left off at Scotland Yard, lulled by a beckoning pension, Jim and his wife rented some land in Somerset from a family trust. Assets at that stage amounted to ten cows, a two-stall milking bail, an old van with a defective gear lever and a caravan, in which the Barnards lived. It was tough-going at first, but they gradually built up the dairy herd and went into partnership with a local farmer, Simon Gooding, who, like them, had been squeezed by EEC milk quotas. While Barnard and Gooding's cattle and goats provided the milk for doorstep deliveries, Jim went back to the States to learn about ice-cream, and to persuade Steve to share with him the secrets of his craft. This he did and Jim returned to Somerset with the winning recipe.

Barnard and Gooding launched their home-grown product in the spring of 1987. Their initial output was one day's production a week which they sold from five bicycles on sea-fronts and in town centres. The response was immediate and staggering. By the end of that summer production was up to three days a week, and in the winter the entire process was intensified. Now they employ ten people full-time and can scarcely cope with demand. They've even been taken up by a local supermarket, where they compete with the established commercial brands.

Why is Jim's ice-cream so popular? The label says it all: 'No artificial anything'. The ingredients are fresh, simple, natural. The strawberry tastes of strawberries, instead of flavouring agents, and there are sizeable flecks of recognisable fruit all over the surface. Similarly, the Cointreau and orange variety is creamy and addictive. I've no doubt the great Steve himself would be proud of his emulator.

Jim Barnard, meanwhile, is prepared to share his experience with others who care about quality. If you'd like to contact him, or if you should find yourself in Somerset and fancy a good ice-cream, here's his address:

Keward Farm,
Pawlett,
Bridgwater,
Somerset TA6 4SE

Initially, Jim's approach was that of an amateur, in the proper sense of the word. Hans Schweitzer, on the other hand, whom we last met at dawn in Cambridge, has always had the single-mindedness of a professional. From his first sight of a chef's hat at the age of fifteen, he has known that cooking is all he wants to do.

For top chefs there are no frontiers. The French language of the kitchen is international, and they must be prepared to work and learn wherever opportunity takes them. After an apprenticeship, a spell at the Munich Hotel School and hard graft in a number of restaurants, Hans was offered a job in Spain. Then it was back to the most renowned hotel school in Germany, at Heidelberg, where he achieved the official title of Maître de Cuisine.

Next stop was the Sheraton in Teheran where, at the age of 25, Hans was appointed Executive Chef, commanding a brigade of 70. Those were the days of the Shah, when parties for 3,000 guests were not uncommon. A symphony orchestra would entertain from a platform actually in the Olympic-sized pool, surrounded by ice carvings. Here the Shah's guests – prime ministers, film stars and glamorous jet-setters – were treated to delicacies such as golden caviar from the albino sturgeon, reserved exclusively for the Shah.

Sometimes there were picnics by the Caspian Sea. Tents and casino tables were flown in from London, and the charcoal grill stretched for 150 metres. Kebabs would marinate for three days with limes, yoghurt, onion juice, herbs and saffron. There was herb-fed lamb stuffed with a long grain rice found only in Iran; sautéed chicken with cranberries and pistachios; braised duck with black cherries; large brioches filled with fresh tuna or lobster and, if the glitterati still had room for them, rosewater sorbets.

Travels through Afghanistan, India, Nepal and Turkey brought Hans Schweitzer to Brussels which shares, with Paris, the highest standard of cuisine in Europe. From there he came to London before heading for Barbados. It was while he was based in the Caribbean that he took part in a gastronomic competition in New Orleans. They made him a freeman of the city, and the cuisine of Louisiana remains a major influence in his cooking.

Back home in Germany, Hans opened his own restaurant at Bad Homburg and within months was awarded a Michelin star. Five years later he and his wife Kathy settled in Cambridge, opening an instantly popular confiserie.

Confiserie, Hans explains, is largely a Swiss concept. As practised by him it embraces pâtisserie as well as sophisticated chocolate confections. His wedding cakes, one of which was seen on *Food and Drink*, have become a local legend, and his handmade chocolates are superb. He says they demand as much skill as any creation of a chef de cuisine.

Although they come from such different backgrounds, Hans Schweitzer and Jim Barnard are united in their dedication to quality. Though neither ice-cream nor confiserie would be recommended by nutritionists on a daily basis as part of a balanced diet, the odd treat is to be recommended. Food, after all, isn't just fuel; it should be fun too. With that in mind, here's Hans' recipe for Chocolate Truffle Gâteau.

CHOCOLATE TRUFFLE GÂTEAU
Serves 10

5 oz (150 g) butter, softened, plus extra for greasing
5 oz (150 g) plain chocolate
5½ oz (165 g) sugar
3 oz (75 g) ground almonds
3 eggs, separated
3½ oz (90 g) plain flour

For the filling:
10 fl oz (300 ml) double cream
7 oz (200 g) plain chocolate
2 oz (50 g) raspberry jam

Pre-heat the oven to 350°F (180°C), gas mark 4. Grease a 9-in (23-cm) diameter sponge mould. Melt the chocolate in the top part of a double saucepan. Beat the softened butter with 3 oz (75 g) sugar until the mixture is fluffy, then fold in the melted chocolate, ground almonds and egg yolks. Beat the egg whites and the rest of the sugar till white and forming peaks, then fold them into the chocolate mixture. Sieve the flour on top and fold it in. Pour into the greased mould and bake for 40 minutes. Allow to cool.

In the meantime, make the chocolate cream filling. Bring the cream to the boil and add the chocolate, broken into small pieces. When the chocolate has melted, stir to a smooth cream. Cool for 1 hour.

Slice the cooled sponge horizontally into three layers. Spread the jam and chocolate cream between the layers. Place together and spread the rest of the chocolate cream smoothly on top. Decorate with chocolate truffles or flakes. Allow to set.

RECIPES
MICHAEL BARRY

In the last series of *Food and Drink*, we were granted a unique interview with Mrs Hudson, cook and housekeeper to Sherlock Holmes. By kind permission of the great detective, she was permitted to regale us with her version of the traditional Victorian Christmas pudding, Plum Duff. We present it with pleasure (and with more than a little help from Fanny Craddock).

PLUM DUFF
Serves 4 to 6

10 oz (275 g) self-raising flour
5 oz (150 g) finely chopped beef suet
6 oz (175 g) sultanas
Pinch of salt

Sift the flour into a basin, and work in the suet and sultanas with a pinch of salt. Make a well in the middle and gradually add about 2 fl oz (50 ml) water. Work the mixture until you have a firm dough, shape this into a ball and enclose it in several buttered greaseproof papers.

Put the ball into a 2-pint (1.2-litre) pudding basin. Cover the basin with kitchen foil, make a pleat in the centre to allow for expansion during cooking, and tie with string just below the lip of the basin. Make a handle with the string to lift the basin out at the end of cooking.

Put the basin into a saucepan about 2 in (5 cm) wider than it, raising the basin on a trivet. Add enough water to reach halfway up the basin. Steam for 2 hours. Keep the water gently boiling, and top up when necessary.

Turn out of the basin, dust the pudding with sugar and serve with cream.

PINEAPPLE AND ALMOND CHEESECAKE
Serves 6

Diabetics have to pay special attention to their diet, so they eat plenty of fresh produce, and less sugar and fat – a healthy, balanced diet from which we could all benefit. By contrast with Mrs Hudson's Plum Duff, the following recipe is a low-fat cheesecake suggested by a dietician at the Aylesbury Diabetic Clinic. She teaches her diabetics how to make this relatively low-calorie pudding as an occasional treat.

For the base:
4 oz (100 g) unsalted low-fat spread
8 oz (225 g) digestive or plain wholemeal biscuits, crushed

For the cheesecake mixture:
4 oz (100 g) unsalted low-fat spread
1 lb (450 g) skimmed milk soft cheese (such as Quark)
1 medium egg, beaten
1 teaspoon almond essence
2 teaspoons sugar-free sweetener
1 oz (25 g) ground almonds
4 oz (100 g) fresh or unsweetened tinned pineapple

To decorate:
5 oz (150 g) fresh or unsweetened tinned pineapple rings

To make the base, melt the low-fat spread in a saucepan over a low heat. Remove from the heat and add the crushed biscuits. Use this mixture to cover the bottom of a 10-in (25-cm) flan dish, and refrigerate to set.

Meanwhile, cream the rest of the low-fat spread with the skimmed milk cheese, egg, almond essence, artificial sweetener, ground almonds and pineapple – either with a food processor or by hand. Top the biscuit base with this and refrigerate for 2 hours. Decorate with the pineapple rings.

Serve, with the happy knowledge that each slice of cheese-cake contains only around 250 calories!

COBBLERS

Fruit cobblers are an ancient country tradition in Britain, and a frugal one, too: a hot baked pudding with a topping made from stale bread. The cut-up bread, waiting to be used and lying in rows like the leather heels in a cobbler's shop, gave the dish its name. Nowadays the topping is usually made of a sponge mixture, but whichever you prefer, here are a couple of tasty fruit fillings.

BLACKBERRY COBBLER
Serves 4 to 6

1 lb (450 g) blackberries, fresh or frozen
5 oz (150 g) caster sugar
1 small bloomer loaf
1 egg
5 fl oz (150 ml) milk
A pinch of allspice
½ teaspoon grated nutmeg

Pre-heat the oven to 350°F (180°C), gas mark 4. Wash or defrost the blackberries, and put them in a 1½-pint (900 ml) pie dish. Mix with 4 oz (100 g) sugar. Cut the bloomer loaf in half across, and, using one of the halves, cut into ½-in (1-cm) thick slices to make the 'cobbles'. Beat the egg and milk with a pinch of allspice, and dip the bread pieces in the mixture.

Place them over the top of the blackberries, carefully overlapping them to form the cobbled effect. Sprinkle with the remaining sugar and the grated nutmeg and bake for 20 minutes, or until golden brown.

PLUM AND APPLE COBBLER
Serves 4 to 6

1 lb (450 g) cooking apples
1 lb (450 g) stoned plums
4 oz (100 g) caster sugar

For the topping:
2 oz (50 g) butter
2 oz (50 g) caster sugar
1 egg
4 oz (100 g) self-raising flour
A pinch of allspice
A little milk

Pre-heat the oven to 350°F (180°C), gas mark 4. Blend the topping ingredients in a food processor, or mix by hand: cream the butter and sugar, slowly add the beaten egg, and fold in the sifted flour and allspice, adding milk to loosen the mixture, if necessary. It should be a thick cream.

Core and peel the cooking apples, and cut these and the plums into thick slices. Stew them in a saucepan with the sugar and water for approximately 5 minutes, until just soft. Drain away two-thirds of the water, and transfer into a 1½-pint (900 ml) pie dish. Cover the fruit with the sponge mixture and bake for 25 to 30 minutes until the topping is crisp and golden.

REAL EGG CUSTARD
Serves 4 to 6

To put the finishing touch to your cobbler, serve it with custard, that great British favourite – but *real* custard, slightly paler than the imitation, slightly less sweet, and infinitely more delicious.

3 egg yolks
2 dessertspoons caster sugar
1 teaspoon cornflour
1 teaspoon vanilla essence
10 fl oz (300 ml) milk

Whisk the egg yolks, sugar, cornflour and vanilla essence. Gently heat the milk, and add to the other ingredients. Whisk and pour into a saucepan. Simmer the custard gently, stirring continuously, until thickened. Pour over your fruit pudding and eat immediately!

CRÈME CARAMEL
Serves 6

Across the Channel they have another version of real custard that has proven endurably popular on this side. For a perfect end to a sophisticated meal, crème caramel – the custard that makes its own sauce – has few competitors.

10 fl oz (300 ml) single cream
10 fl oz (300 ml) milk
2 tablespoons vanilla sugar
(or 2 tablespoons caster sugar and a few drops vanilla essence)
2 eggs and 1 egg yolk
2 tablespoons granulated sugar

Pre-heat the oven to 300°F (150°C), gas mark 2. Gently heat the milk and cream with the vanilla sugar until dissolved, taking care not to bring the mixture to the boil. Cool slightly, then beat the eggs and whisk them into the mixture. In a separate saucepan dissolve the granulated sugar and 1 tablespoon of water, and heat until the solution thickens and turns golden brown. Do not overboil.

Pour the caramel into 6 small ramekins. Allow to cool, then strain the custard mixture onto the caramel through a sieve. Place in a bain marie or roasting dish filled with water halfway up the ramekins and bake for 45 to 50 minutes. Remove from the oven and leave to cool. To turn out, loosen the edges with a palette knife, put a small plate over the top and turn over, giving the bottom of the ramekin a sharp tap to loosen the caramel.

HOME-MADE ICE-CREAM
Serves 4 to 6

I first discovered this ice-cream in a Chinese take-away. It's foolproof, needs no special equipment, contains no crunchy bits of ice and tastes fabulous.

3 whole eggs
3 tablespoons icing sugar
5 fl oz (150 ml) double cream
1 teaspoon vanilla essence

Whisk the eggs until they are lemon-coloured, frothy and thick. Whisk in the sugar, spoonful by spoonful, until it is all absorbed. In a separate bowl beat the cream until it is thick but not stiff. Add the vanilla to the egg mixture, and then fold in the cream gently, so you don't knock all the air out.

At this stage you can add up to 5 oz (150 g) crushed fruit or other flavourings. Strawberries, peaches, strong coffee, and chocolate are my favourites. Pour into a container and freeze for at least 4 hours. The ice-cream does not need stirring, but benefits from 30 minutes softening in the refrigerator before serving.

Jill Goolden's suggestions for sweet dessert wines

In contrast to recent years, a revival of sweet wines is now taking place. They are excellent with puddings, so do try them.

Muscat de Beaumes-de-Venise: leads the revival. You can order it by the glass in many restaurants. From the Rhône region in France, its sweetness is the result of the fermentation having stopped before all the sugar in the sweet grape juice has been converted into alcohol. It is then fortified with spirit, so it is quite powerful (around 16%). Beware!

Asti Spumante: a delicious Italian sparkling wine, particularly good with cake. Around half the alcoholic strength of Muscat de Beaumes-de-Venise and available at a lower price.

Moscato Spumante: another sparkling wine from Italy, still lower in alcoholic strength. It comes from a less distinguished area than Asti, hence it is lower in price.

These three wines have a fruity and aromatic flavour, which comes from the distinctive Muscat grape. If you have ever eaten delicious muscatel raisins, you will recognise the flavour – they, too, are the same grape.

MARMALADE

On a final sweet note, I offer my thoughts on marmalade in tribute to many happy moments with toast. For most of us, making jam or marmalade is a dream of the rural 'good life'; far from reality. It needn't be; my wife – a world-class maker of marmalade – has taught me a crafty way to do it. You can use either ordinary caster sugar or preserving sugar, or there is a new kind of sugar available with added pectin – the setting agent in fruit – which gives an extra insurance against ending up with a runny syrup.

4 lb (1.75 kg) citrus fruit, such as Seville oranges, grapefruit,
lemons and pomelos
4 lb (1.75 kg) caster sugar, preserving sugar or the new kind of sugar
now available with added pectin

Squeeze the citrus fruits, reserving the rinds and pips. Put the juice into a large, heavy-bottomed aluminium saucepan, or special preserving pan, which has been cleaned and sterilised before use. Put the pips into a muslin bag and tie it up. Cut the rind into fine strips. Add the bag, the rind and 2 to 2½ pints (1.2 to 1.5 litres) of water to the saucepan. Bring to the boil, and simmer for an hour, or until translucent. Remove the muslin bag, and add the sugar. Bring to the boil, and stir until all the sugar is dissolved.

Boil for a further 20 to 40 minutes, checking regularly for setting. Put a small amount of marmalade onto a saucer which has been in the fridge. If it sets quickly on the saucer it is ready. Do not overboil.

Decant the marmalade into sterilised jars. Fill the jars up to the top, put a disc of waxed or greaseproof paper over the top, and seal tightly. Wipe the outsides of the jars, if necessary, to remove any drips.

Seville oranges

Once only the oranges grown in or near Seville in Spain could be called Sevilles. But it's now the name given to all bitter oranges. Most still come from Spain and their combination of bitter-sweetness and high pectin levels make them the ideal fruit for marmalade, either on their own or combined with other citrus fruits, or even with rhubarb or ginger. They come into the shops after Christmas and are available through till April.

Seville oranges are one of the few fruits still not to be treated with a fungicide wax coating. But if you are using other citrus fruits for marmalade, the Ministry of Agriculture assure us that the tiny amounts involved are safe.

SOFT OPTIONS

ORANGE SQUASH
JILL GOOLDEN

You might imagine that, when shopping in a supermarket, I concentrate my attentions on the wine department, but I'm much more likely to be found in the soft drinks aisle, agonising over the many rows of orange squash. I'm paying the penalty of crimes past; of gross negligence I had no idea I was guilty of until I was forced to become a 'regular' in the soft drinks aisle. When each of my babies was born, I was advised by the health visitor that, as well as feeding them myself, I should give them water from a bottle. This was a challenge that, despite my best intentions, I was unable to meet. For a start, the babies found London tap water a shocking let-down after mother's milk, and then, having reached the age of reason at about six weeks, they each decided there was no point in accepting anything at all from a bottle.

Mercifully, they soon reached the age – at about six months old – when they could grab a mug. Now was the moment to wean them on to water, so I thought. Of course, they had also developed a pair of bellows for lungs and some extremely powerful vocal cords. And the first sip of water from the mug immediately brought both into action simultaneously. I am still waiting for the day when I can persuade either of my daughters to drink plain water from the tap. To be fair (to me that is) babies are conditioned to like flavour: ordinary water is simply too dull for them. Meanwhile I am driven to buy the purest flavouring I can find which can be used in minute quantity to transform water into something acceptable.

Fresh fruit juices, such as fresh-pressed English apple juice, heavily diluted, feature powerfully in our lives. But there is a need in the store cupboard, too, for good old orange squash. Conscious of past allegations against squashes (for instance tartrazine, a colouring agent identifiable as E102, widely used in orange drinks, has been linked with hyperactivity), I know I must spend time studying the labels, making up for my past sins of omission.

The Food and Drugs Act 1964 laid down a code (due to be revised) regulating the form of words manufacturers can use to describe their orange drinks on the label. Essentially, there are four different categories of orange drink that can be diluted with water. The principal difference between them is the percentage and type of real orange each contains.

Whole Orange Drink
Isn't wholly orange, but instead contains whole oranges. This means the real juice content is derived from the total orange: skin, pith, pips, flesh, juice, the lot, in a 'comminuted' form. And a drink calling itself 'Whole Orange Drink' need contain only a minimum of 2% comminuted oranges in the concentrate. Many drinks contain more, but the percentage of 'whole orange' is never more than 25%.

Orange Squash
Has, by law, to contain a minimum of 25% fruit juice in concentrated form, that is, before dilution.

High-juice Squash
Is generally accepted to have a minimum of 40% fruit juice or fruit juice and comminuted orange in concentrated form. When diluted with water, however, even a high, high juice would have less than 15% fruit content in the glass.

Concentrated Fruit Juice
Must contain 100% concentrated fruit juice.

There are many more variables; colour is one. At the purest end of the colour scale are drinks with no added colour at all. Others claim boldly to have 'no artificial colours', and the accent here is on the word 'artificial' because they probably do have *added* colours, albeit natural ones. Beta-carotene (E160a), derived not from the orange, but from the carrot, is one example; Annatto (E160b), which may cause allergic reactions, is another. When we put a range of diluted orange drinks together for a comparative tasting, the colour spectrum ranged from lime green at the wishy-washy end, to brilliant day-glow orange.

Sugar content varies too. As well as natural fructose already present in the fruit juice, there is added sugar (probably sucrose, derived from sugar cane). All drinks not claiming to be low calorie must contain at least 8 oz (225 g) of added sugar to each litre bottle. When you take the sugar already present in the juice into account, this works out at 1½ teaspoonfuls of sugar in a glass of diluted orange. The sugar content is not always expressed as a percentage, which is unhelpful.

Not long ago much publicity was given to stories about children's teeth rotting to little stumps from the pernicious sugar in fruit drinks, and all the medical evidence points an unswerving finger at sugar as a chief cause of tooth decay. Sugar is certainly conspicuously present in fruit drinks and squashes, but the major dental damage in these shock-horror cases was caused by extremely sugary drinks being given to infants in a bottle, particularly when it was left in the baby's mouth for some time as a dummy substitute. It was not caused simply by drinking fruit drinks, although a sugary drink can coat a child's teeth as it passes through the mouth, even when dispensed from a mug. It is always a good idea to dilute fruit drinks as much as possible; a little squash can, if you are firm, go a loooong way. There are also low-cal orange drinks with 'no added sugar'. This doesn't mean they have no added sweeteners; certainly they do – artificial ones, particularly aspartame and saccharin.

As for vitamin C, you might expect the drinks with a higher juice content to have a higher content of this essential vitamin, but in fact most of it is destroyed in the making of the drink. In some instances, vitamin C (or ascorbic acid as it is otherwise known, additive E300) is put back in, partly for you, and partly as a preservative. One orange drink, C-Vit, claims to provide much of your daily requirement of vitamins in each 3-tablespoon serving – 100% requirement of vitamin C, 50% of vitamin B and 17% each of vitamin D, niacin and calcium.

Agonising over labels, contents and additives is confined to grown-ups, who don't consume the lion's share of the squash. To get an accurate picture of the actual flavour of the various products on offer, unjaded by adult prejudice, we invited troops of Brownies and Cubs (with their minders) into the studio to taste a number of drinks in each orange-drink category. We ended up with a kids' panel and a grown-up panel – and there wasn't much agreement between the two!

Authenticity and similarity to the original fruit from which the drink is supposed to derive was not a critical factor for the children – far from it. The more artificial, the more like sweets, in fact, the drink tasted, the higher it scored. The drink that gained the most points from the Cubs and Brownies was a 'whole orange drink', that is, one from the category requiring the smallest proportion of original fruit.

'Tastes like Refreshers,' said James Mercer from the Blueberry pack in Oxfordshire, giving it his highest score (he also, incidentally, identified it as Kia-Ora). Michael Parks, also of the Blueberry pack, thought his favourite drink tasted 'like sherbet – it's very nice'; while Katy Brydon, a Brownie from High Wycombe, chose as her top drink a high-juice squash, praising it for looking 'like sea water', smelling of 'nothing' and tasting 'beautiful'.

The same drinks on my scoring sheet were rated as follows: 'Thoroughly unnatural colour. Smells like off fruit; sugary but fresh tasting. Unpleasant aftertaste.' And for the whole orange drink: 'Looks milky green, tastes of oranges though too sweet. Fruity rather than chemically.' Worst of all were the drinks with artificial sweeteners, which got the thumbs-down from both panels. The children thought they tasted 'plasticky' and 'rubbery', while the long-suffering adults considered them a dead loss. I thought they had an obvious sweet-and-sour taste, verging on the bitter, the kind of taste that makes you thirsty rather than quenches your thirst.

Concentrated orange drinks offered a bit of light relief to the adult tasters on the taste front, but most concentrated orange drinks would inflict serious injury on the pocket. One actually cost more, measure for measure, than standard carton orange juices. Even these concentrated 100% juices have a manufactured flavour. So, if you want a reasonably economical orange drink, what can you do? You can make your own.

THE FOOD AND DRINK ORANGE SQUASH
Drink this very fresh, preferably on the day you make it.

8 juicy oranges, such as Israeli Shamouti oranges, thoroughly washed
4 tablespoons caster sugar

Squeeze all the oranges and reserve the juice. Slice the peel and place it in a saucepan with 2 pints (1.2 litres) of water, and any pulp remaining in the squeezer. Bring to the boil for 20 minutes. Let the peel cool and then strain through a fine mesh. Add enough boiling water to the orange liquid to make it up to 2 pints (1.2 litres). Mix together the juice and liquid and stir in the sugar. Leave to cool and refrigerate.

Putting my home-made version to the test, I diffidently offered it to James Mercer, the Cub who had so brilliantly identified (blind) one of the orange drinks. Evidently having studied tasting form in detail, he raised the glass, swirled, sniffed, tasted, gargled and swallowed, before pronouncing it to be very nice, in fact, the best of the lot. This was gratifying, and restored my belief that true quality – that of the fresh-pressed orange, in this case – will out.

NOT SO SOFT AN OPTION

Making drinks was an interesting and occasionally hazardous feature of my childhood. In East Sussex, where we lived, there were few households without a ginger beer plant churning away rather disgustingly in the larder. The plant part was 'live', like a live yoghurt, and, fed regularly on ginger and sugar, looked very much as though it had a life of its own, undulating like a sand-coloured sea monster. There was a kind of swap-shop of ginger beer plants in the neighbourhood: if yours died or exhausted itself, you could borrow a section of someone else's and start again. After a few weeks in buckets, the resultant ginger beer would be bottled, and this was hazardous, for occasionally the bottles would pop.

At the time, I don't remember questioning the reason for this, but now that I am older and wiser, I know. We were actually making something really quite alcoholic. Bottled with the active yeast and sugar still present, the fermentation would continue, creating CO_2, which gave it a nice fizziness, if we caught it in time, and occasionally built up enough pressure to burst the bottle.

Now that making country and kit wines is such a popular pastime (see pages 35 to 42) all sorts of sophisticated gadgetry is available which can prevent you from having similar casualties on the ginger beer front. The recipe below does not involve a ginger beer plant. It is as alcoholic as ordinary beer, so do follow all the instructions carefully and watch out. Exploding bottles can be dangerous. All the equipment can be obtained from Boots' wine and beer-making departments, or from specialist shops.

GINGER BEER
Makes 14 to 16 pints

1 lb (450 g) granulated sugar
Rind and juice of 2 lemons
1 oz (25 g) bruised, chopped fresh root of ginger
½ oz (15 g) cream of tartar
1 large tablespoon brewer's yeast

Sterilise a fermenting bin or white plastic bucket with sterilising solution or tablets. Rinse it thoroughly. (Don't use a coloured bucket as the alcohol will draw out the poisonous pigment.) Put all the ingredients, except the yeast, in the bin, then add 2 gallons of boiling water. Stir to dissolve the sugar. Leave until the water is hand-warm, then add the yeast. Cover the bin and put it in the warmest place you can find.

Skim the liquid of any yeasty froth every 24 hours. After 3 days test the liquid with a hydrometer to check whether fermentation has finished. Fill a tall glass or hydrometer jar with the liquid and let the hydrometer float in that until it settles. The liquid must settle at the 1.010 mark, or between 1.010 and 1.000. It is extremely important to take this reading to avoid any explosions after bottling. Just keep checking the liquid until it reaches the right stage. Strain the liquid into sterilised plastic (not glass) bottles, add an extra teaspoon of sugar per bottle, screw the caps on tightly and leave in a cold place for 3 days before drinking. The ginger beer should be drunk within a fortnight.

GINGER BEER CORDIAL
A delicious non-alcoholic version can be made even more simply. Highly gingery and fairly sweet, it mixes well with soda water.

2 oz (50 g) root ginger, bruised, peeled and chopped
1 lb (450 g) granulated sugar
½ oz (15 g) tartaric acid
2 lemons – the juice of one and the other sliced

Put the ginger, sugar, tartaric acid and lemon into a bowl and cover with 1 gallon of boiling water. Stir until the sugar has dissolved. Leave for 3 to 4 days. Strain and bottle. It will be ready to drink after a few days and can be diluted with either still or sparkling water.

UNCLE SAM'S KITCHEN

INTRODUCTION
MICHAEL BARRY

When I explain my enthusiasm for American food (American as in USA, that is) most people greet my protestations with anything from polite amusement to blatant contempt. If only they knew how wrong they were! Their commonly held view is partly the result of America's own success in selling her cinema image: the brilliantly constructed 'adman's' dreams of teenagers in hot rods living on junk foods, often eaten without first removing the chewing gum, are pervasive and worldwide. But they are false, and even the worst excesses of diet are relatively recent. The American hamburger was first put in a bun early this century, and it was only in Los Angeles in the 1920s, at the time that Hollywood was becoming the world's entertainment centre, that pickles, tomato, lettuce and 'mayo' were added.

Across America, but especially in the eastern seaboard states from New England in the North, to Louisiana in the South, there is a tradition of fine and robust cooking going back hundreds of years. It is a tradition that often recalls, better than their native lands, the original dishes of the settlers who made America their home. And the traditions could hardly be more varied. Into the old Spanish colony of Florida came the French to add their influence, then the English, and all the time most of the cooking itself was being done by black slaves or servants brought from all over Africa, who added their own touches. The result is the justly famous Creole cuisine with its gumbos, fabulous fish dishes, and the meal it gave to the world – brunch: after jazz, New Orleans' most famous export. All the way up the coast are other delicacies: Southern or Maryland fried chicken; candied sweet potatoes for Thanksgiving dinner in Virginia; superb Italian peasant cooking made with millionaires' ingredients on the lower East Side of New York. New England has its lobsters, clams, codfish, Rhode Island chickens, chowders, cranberries... the list is endless.

The other notable thing about American food is that much of it is literally home grown; that is, made with ingredients originating in the New World. When the Pilgrim Fathers were starving, the Indians fed them with potatoes, turkey, corn and beans. All had been grown by the Indians themselves. And in the American larder or greengrocery there still waited tomatoes, pumpkins, marrows, avocados, chocolate, sweet potatoes, sweet and chili peppers – all the native Americans' gift to the world, having been developed for over 3,000 years in the land we now think of as Mexico.

Today, America's wealth, its wide range of climate and geography, plus its mastery of food production, mean that almost every foodstuff known to man, from pineapples to pink salmon, olive oil to oysters, is produced there. The raw materials are superb and, outside the confines of the fast-food emporia, they are used with imagination and conviction. And even the way the all-American foods and drinks have become the world's standard in fast food – burgers, fries and colas – demonstrate that at mass-market level American food is universally appealing and accessible.

Flavour-intensive, exuberant, varied and exciting... why not try some of the taste sensations from Uncle Sam's kitchen for yourself?

SALT BEEF SANDWICHES

The most recent slice of American culture to have hit these shores has been American football. The gladiatorial rushes of its body-armoured teams of giants culminate each year in the Superbowl – four hours of nail-biting action that require the frequent refuelling of its 60 million television spectators. Salt beef sandwiches are the popular choice, just beating hot dogs as instant energy food. Salt, or 'corned', beef (not to be confused with the tinned corned beef product enjoyed in this country) has been eaten in the North East United States since the days of the settlers; the arrival of the Irish immigrants in the last century gave it renewed popularity. It's good hot, sliced with cabbage, or reheated as the famous corned beef hash.

A piece of silverside or brisket, ready salted
6 juniper berries
6 peppercorns
1 bay leaf
4 cloves
A few coriander seeds

Put everything in a pressure cooker or large saucepan. If using a pressure cooker, add 1 pint (600 ml) water and cook for 20 minutes per lb. To cook in an ordinary saucepan, cover with water and cook for 1 hour per lb. Remove from the pan, drain the water and slice the meat while hot. Serve it sandwiched in light rye or soft-grain white bread, with dill pickles (gherkins), American mustard, crinkle-cut crisps and hot potato salad.

HOT POTATO SALAD
Serves 4

1 lb (450 g) freshly boiled potatoes
1 tablespoon cider vinegar
½ teaspoon salt
4 tablespoons mayonnaise (see page 51)
1 bunch spring onions, finely chopped

Chop the boiled potatoes and sprinkle with the cider vinegar and salt. Stir in the mayonnaise and chopped spring onions. Serve hot.

NEW ENGLAND FISH CHOWDER
Serves 4

This thick New England soup goes back five or six generations. (The corn chowder on page 61 is a vegetarian version of the same tradition.) Individual recipes reflect the availability of ingredients, especially during winter, when little fresh food was to be had: consequently shellfish, always to be fished from the shores, especially clams, were often used. Here is an equally venerable version of chowder, made with the fish that first made Boston wealthy, the cod.

1 lb (450 g) cod fillet, skinned
1 cup cracker or savoury biscuit crumbs
8 oz (225 g) onion, finely chopped
4 oz (100 g) butter
1 lb (450 g) peeled potatoes
1 pint (600 ml) milk
Salt and pepper
Parsley, chopped

Cut the cod into 1-in (2.5-cm) squares. Fry half the crumbs and the onion gently in 2 oz (50 g) butter. Cut the potato into ½-in (1-cm) dice and boil gently in the milk. When the potato is just cooked – about 10 minutes – add the fish, onion mixture, rest of the butter, salt and pepper. Simmer for 5 minutes more. To serve, spoon into bowls and sprinkle over the remaining crumbs and a little parsley.

SPAGHETTI AND MEATBALLS
Serves 4 to 6
The people who emigrated to America at the turn of the century were – in the famous words of the sign over Ellis Island – the tired and the poor. In America, they found a better life, which gave them the wealth to transform their diets. They kept, though, their taste for highly seasoned and robust flavours. This was especially true of the Italian immigrants who settled in New York and Boston.

For the meatballs:
1 lb (450 g) minced beef
1 onion, finely chopped
2 slices bread, soaked in milk
2 oz (50 g) Parmesan cheese, grated
1 teaspoon dried oregano
1 teaspoon dried thyme
Oil for frying

For the sauce:
1 lb (450 g) leeks, washed
2 tablespoons olive oil
1 × 14-oz (400-g) tin Italian tomatoes
2 tablespoons tomato purée
1 teaspoon dried basil
1 teaspoon dried oregano

1 lb (450 g) long Italian spaghetti

Mix the meatball ingredients and knead until firm. Roll into 12 balls and fry gently until brown. Cut the washed leeks into ½-in (1-cm) slices and sauté in olive oil for 2 minutes. Add the other sauce ingredients, mash them together to blend and simmer for 20 minutes. Add the meatballs and simmer for another 10 minutes.

Cook the spaghetti in a big pan of boiling water for 3 minutes, take it off the heat, cover and leave for 7 minutes. Drain the spaghetti, pile in a big serving dish, pour the sauce and meatballs over, and serve. You can offer more Parmesan cheese to sprinkle over.

SOUTHERN FRIED CHICKEN
Serves 4

There are as many versions of this recipe as there are cooks who can claim to be Southern. My crafty version doesn't use breadcrumbs, but you can use them to coat the chicken, with a little egg brushed on first, and still be perfectly authentic. Either way, you get moist, juicy chicken inside a really crisp coating. In the Southern States this would be served with corn fritters, sautéed sliced bananas and plenty of mashed potato.

1 jointed roasting chicken
2 tablespoons lemon juice
1 teaspoon powdered cinnamon
4 tablespoons flour, seasoned with paprika and bay leaf
Vegetable oil, for shallow frying
5 fl oz (150 ml) milk or single cream

Rub the chicken joints with the lemon juice and cinnamon, and dip in 3 tablespoonfuls of seasoned flour. Put ¼ in (5 mm) oil in a big frying pan that has a lid. Heat the oil until it is just below smoking and put in the chicken. Brown on all sides, and turn the heat down. Cover the pan and cook for 20 minutes, turning once. Remove the chicken to a serving dish, pour off all the oil and add 1 tablespoon of the seasoned flour to the pan. Cook, stirring, until brown, then pour in the milk or cream and stir again to make a smooth gravy. Serve with the chicken.

CRANBERRY SAUCE

The annual cranberry harvest in Massachusetts is one of the sights of the New England fall. The countryside is ablaze with the colour of the dying leaves, and the salt marshes where the cranberries grow are flooded. The cranberries fall into the water, and a crimson tide sweeps acres of fruit-laden water through the sluices. It was these berries that made the sauce that accompanied the earliest settlers' Thanksgiving (and now the Christmas) turkey. Some of the earliest cranberry sauces were uncooked but modern tastes prefer this bright, tart and refreshing cooked preserve.

1 lb (450 g) cranberries
4 oz (100 g) caster sugar
2 tablespoons orange juice
Grated rind of ½ orange
1 teaspoon butter

Put the berries, sugar and juice in a small pan and bring to the boil. Simmer gently for 10 minutes while the cranberries pop, making sure they don't catch and burn. Add the orange rind and butter and simmer for another 5 minutes. Cool and store in the refrigerator until served.

A lovely Scandinavian sauce, made of cloudberries (similar to cranberries, which can be used instead), substitutes a thinly sliced, peeled pear for the orange rind. Make sure the pear is ripe. Serve this with cold turkey.

CANDIED SWEET POTATOES
Serves 4

Sweet potatoes are a peculiarly American vegetable, although they are now grown all around the world, and are widely available here in ethnic food markets. They are delicious baked in their skins and eaten with butter, salt and pepper; they also make gratins and good soups. But what roast potatoes are to special occasions in Britain, candied sweet potatoes are in the States, especially at Thanksgiving.

1½ lb (750 g) sweet potatoes
2 tablespoons soft brown sugar
½ teaspoon nutmeg
½ teaspoon cinnamon
2 oz (50 g) butter

Wash the potatoes thoroughly and cut them as necessary to make even-sized pieces. Boil for 20 minutes, drain, and peel. Slice the potatoes into 1-in (2.5-cm) rounds and lay them in a single close layer in a baking dish. Sprinkle the sugar and spices over, dot with butter, and grill or bake until the sugar has melted and the topping is bubbling. Served traditionally with turkey, these are good with any plain meat.

CREOLE CHICKEN GUMBO
Serves 4
Gumbo is the not-very-appetising name for the classic aromatic stews of that most gastronomic American city, New Orleans. It's a dish with mixed African, Spanish and French origins, so it justly represents the cosmopolitan cuisine of Louisiana. There are two quite different ways to make a gumbo. The first requires dried, powdered, sassafras root, or 'file', which I've never found outside the States, as a thickening agent. But the tropical seed pod, okra, is equally suitable and luckily is widely available here, especially in shops or supermarkets catering to an ethnic community. Serve chicken gumbo in bowls, with plenty of white rice.

1 jointed roasting chicken
Vegetable oil, for shallow frying
1 lb (450 g) onions
1 lb (450 g) red and green peppers, mixed
8 oz (225 g) okra
1 × 14-oz (400-g) tin peeled tomatoes
2 garlic cloves, chopped
1 teaspoon dried thyme
½ teaspoon chili powder
Salt and pepper

Fry the chicken pieces lightly in a deep frying pan in a little oil. Clean all the fresh vegetables, and cut them across into ¼-in (5-mm) slices. Add to the chicken, with the tomatoes, the chopped garlic, thyme and chili powder. Add just enough water to cover the chicken, season and simmer, uncovered, for 35 minutes. Serve over cooked white rice.

KEY LIME PIE
Serves 4 to 6
This is Florida's tropical answer to the trans-American favourite, lemon meringue pie. And because this is America, it is sometimes known as 'mile-high' key lime pie: a pie shell filled with a sweet

and sharp fruit filling and topped with a cloud of meringue up to 12 in (30 cm) high. You can make it with just a couple of inches of meringue and still cause quite a stir. Limes are widely available in Britain in greengrocers and supermarkets which specialise in a wide range of tropical fruits.

'Key' is the name for the string of a hundred or more islands that form a chain from Miami across the Caribbean down to Key West, halfway to the Bahamas. They used to grow limes on them, or so they say.

You'll need an 8-in (20-cm) pie shell of shortcrust pastry which should have been baked blind for 10 to 12 minutes.

For the filling:

4 eggs
Juice of 3 limes
1 × 12-oz (350-g) tin condensed milk
½ teaspoon cream of tartar
4 tablespoons caster sugar

Pre-heat the oven to 350°F (180°C), gas mark 4.

Separate the eggs and whisk the yolks with the lime juice and condensed milk until thick. Add 1 stiffly beaten egg white and pour into the pie shell. Make the meringue by whisking the rest of the egg whites with the cream of tartar until they are really stiff. Whisk in all but 1 teaspoon of sugar, a spoonful at a time, until it's absorbed and the meringue is shiny. Pile onto the filling and fork it up into peaks. Sprinkle on the remaining sugar and bake for 30 minutes or until the meringue starts to turn golden. Cool on a rack for at least 3 hours before serving.

SUPERCOOK '88

INTRODUCTION
CHRIS KELLY

Food and Drink combined with the *Sunday Express* Magazine to organise Supercook '88 – a national competition for enthusiastic amateurs. Contestants were invited to send in recipes for a family meal (which might include children) of at least two courses.

The response was amazing. Seven hundred and fifty detailed menus came winging back from all over the British Isles. From these, the judges had the mouth-watering, but otherwise unenviable task, of picking six semi-finalists. It was surprising just how revealing the replies were, both of care given to planning, balance and originality; and of the writers' attitudes to food and its preparation.

Take Judy Aitken for example. Until I read her letter, it had never occurred to me that dishes might have genders. (Eat your heart out, Sigmund Freud!) Judy explained why she chose a pudding called Angel's Hair to follow her venison stew: 'In texture and colour it looks delicate and feminine in comparison with the masculine main course.' And she writes of the deer 'feeling at home with wild rowan and elderberries'. Here, plainly, was a cook with great affection for, and sympathy with, her ingredients.

Judy Aitken was among the half-dozen semi-finalists, five of whom came from Scotland or the North of England. None was from the prosperous Home Counties, although all were brought to London for the acid test where, in the hospitable kitchens of the Hotel Meridien, they would be asked to turn theory into practice and cook their chosen menus. A discerning panel, among them

Food and Drink producer Peter Bazalgette, writer Caroline Conran and chef David Chambers, had to select the three finalists from this formidable line-up:

Judy Aitken

Brought up in Perthshire; an ancestor was a French chef, Maître Pennett, who, in the mid-eighteenth century, came over to cook for the Duke of Northumberland. Judy's a Publicity Assistant for the National Trust of Scotland. The first 'plushy, lushy' cookery book that influenced her was by Robert Carrier. She's been to evening classes at an Edinburgh cookery school, and she and her husband, an architect ('it's incredible how many architects are good cooks'), like to prepare meals together. Judy's speciality: scallops. She's intensely proud of Scotland's wealth of marvellous meat and fish, and was 'thrilled to be flying the flag for Scotland' in the competition.

Rev. John Fernley

Unitarian Minister in Manchester. The food was so abysmal at the Unitarian College where he trained, that he took over the kitchen, introducing fresh ingredients to replace packets. His interest in cooking developed when he began his ministry. There were various phases – Chinese, Indian, French – but above all he's keen on traditional British dishes. John likes to buy what's good in Bolton market and then decide what to make. Specialities: pigeon, venison, duck. Thinks the British are prejudiced against fish: 'You have to win them over.' John enjoys the element of 'surprise and joy' in cooking. He is also an owner of, and writer about, motorcycles.

Vicki Lawson-Brown

Born in Newcastle, now lives in Pity Me, Co. Durham, where she works as a Child Guidance Counsellor. She is an experienced competitor and was twice Northern Cook of the Year. She bemoans the fact that anything remotely unusual – wild mushrooms, sweetbreads, even fresh herbs – is hard to come by in the North East and lays in supplies on regular visits to France, where she taught English for a year as part of her course at Stirling University, and where she plans to live. Vicki confesses that she enters competitions because she enjoys the recognition they bring.

Margaret Loh
Born in Toronto, her father was Chinese, her mother Indonesian. ('My mother can't stand cooking. It's the thing she hates most in life.') At the age of seven, Margaret began making breakfast with her twin sister, later graduating to lunch. She went to boarding school in Wales where she mastered apple crumble and custard. By the time she gained her Ph.D. at Cambridge she thought nothing of cooking for parties of a hundred. Margaret now does research at the Royal Signals Radar Establishment in Malvern. She's a vegetarian, but cooks meat dishes for her husband. She believes food should be prepared fast so it doesn't become boring.

Marjorie Smedley
Retired GP. Born in Scotland. Studied Medicine at St Andrews. Her mother and her grandmother were good cooks. Now Marjorie herself is a grandmother. She travelled with her husband to Trinidad ('blissful and utterly hilarious') when he was advising the CARICOM countries on food production and marketing, and thoroughly enjoyed this gastronomic melting pot of Creole, Chinese, Indian, African influences. Marjorie also spent two years in Washington – 'a cultural desert for food' – and now lives in a 'totally decrepit' farmhouse in Warwickshire. How did she adapt to hotel stoves? 'The heat was the greatest shock. It was like hitting a brick wall.' But 'the dear little sous-chefs [provided to help the contestants] were absolute gems'.

William Watters
After Art School, he served in the Royal Navy for fourteen years, then became a struggling portrait-painter in Plymouth. He used to collect two shillings each from friends to buy scrag end of mutton and spices, and hold curry parties. He lived in Helsinki before hitchhiking to India, where, for two years, he studied to be a Buddhist monk. Now works as Publicity Manager for a toy company in Cheshire. He regards cooking as 'painting on a plate'; his speciality: seafood. William's reaction to the kitchens of the Meridien? 'The scale bowled me over.'

The judges eventually chose Vicki Lawson-Brown, Margaret Loh and Marjorie Smedley to go forward to the final in Paris. There the challenge was even stiffer. The successful trio were each given a measly 100 francs (about £10) with which to buy the ingredients for a two-course meal for two people. They then had to cook the ingredients in the kitchens of the Paris Meridien.

The hotel's Maître Chef, the splendidly named Monsieur Brazier, didn't do much for the finalists' confidence when he intimated that for 100 francs you could hardly hope to feed a dog. Fortunately, he was proved wrong. Let loose in the magnificent street markets, Margaret, Vicki and Marjorie cleared the first hurdle in great style. Margaret, well used to thrift as a student, even had enough change to buy a third course. Vicki had the courage to ask a stallholder, in fluent French, to drop his price. Politely but firmly she was informed that he wasn't running a charity. Marjorie had a moment of crisis when she realised that she'd blown 60 per cent of her budget on a sea trout, but soon recovered. If anything, the greatest problem in the markets was not shortage of cash but the sheer choice on offer. The variety, freshness and appeal of the seafood, meat, game, vegetables, fruit and cheese was almost overwhelming. Add to that the insistent presence of a film crew constantly zooming in on your indecision and you have a recipe for panic.

However, our three finalists were still remarkably cheerful as they took up their stations in the cavernous kitchen of the Meridien. With just two hours to whip up their bid for the title, they once again got to grips with the fierce heat of a hotel range. There's no question of regulating these huge hotplates with a dainty switch. You simply control the rate of cooking by moving the pans on and off. Hovering vigilantly were our eminent judges: Monsieur Brazier, Michael Barry, Keith Floyd and Angela Galbraith, representing the *Sunday Express* Magazine. Keith would dart in and out of the action periodically, offering solace. Resplendent in bow tie, braces and suede shoes, he resembled a mischievous major on a night out in the sergeants' mess. When he offered Marjorie a drink as she stuffed her sea trout, she looked momentarily scandalised, but accepted his kind offer nonetheless. Meanwhile Michael Barry honed to a fine art his ability to scrutinise food at three hundred paces through a pair of spectacles that have seen heavy duty in many a British food market.

At 7.00 pm time was up. The judges sat to deliberate. Each dish was tasted, discussed and awarded marks. Messrs Barry and Floyd were slightly disappointed, and made the valid criticism that, by and large, the contestants hadn't used their opportunities to the fullest. Here on their doorstep was a world of variety, freshness and flavour probably unsurpassed in Europe, yet this was not altogether reflected in the contestants' menus. It was generally agreed, however, that in unfamiliar circumstances they had managed extremely well – and that watching is always a great deal easier than taking part.

The result was close-run. By a whisker, though, the title Supercook '88 finally went to Vicki Lawson-Brown; yet another success to add to her rapidly growing collection. It was a great boost, too, for creative cooking in the North East; a region which, as Vicki testifies, has been slower than most to join the national revival of interest in good food.

Here is a flavour of the competition with the recipes submitted by the six semi-finalists who emerged from the field of 750.

JUDY AITKEN

The 'Angel's Hair' was chosen to complement the rich venison stew. In texture and colour the pudding looks delicate and feminine in comparison to the masculine main course! I chose venison because Scotland – and indeed Britain – has so many local delicacies. I thought the deer would feel 'at home' with wild rowan and elderberries. The pumpkin is a spectacular vessel in which to serve this concoction – a presentation to please the eye and, hopefully, whet one's appetite.

VENISON STEW SERVED IN A PUMPKIN
Serves 6

3 lb (1.5 kg) stewing venison
Seasoned flour
2 oz (50 g) butter
3 tablespoons oil
1 lb (450 g) button onions, peeled
2 stalks celery, sliced
2 carrots, scraped and sliced
2 fat garlic cloves, crushed
8 oz (225 g) tomatoes, peeled and roughly chopped
1 bay leaf
½ teaspoon allspice
½ teaspoon ground mace
1 tablespoon crushed juniper berries
Salt and pepper
2 tablespoons rowan jelly
10 fl oz (300 ml) venison stock
10 fl oz (300 ml) port
2 tablespoons wine vinegar
1 large, flat-bottomed pumpkin – say 7 lb (3 kg)

Pre-heat the oven to 300°F (150°C), gas mark 2.

Dust the venison with seasoned flour. Heat the butter and oil in a frying pan and gently fry the onions for a few minutes. Add the celery, carrots and garlic and fry for a further 5 minutes until lightly browned. Remove the vegetables and fry the meat in several batches in the remaining fat, adding a little extra oil if necessary. Put the cooked vegetables, venison and chopped tomatoes in the casserole, then season with herbs and spices, salt and pepper. Stir in the rowan jelly. Bring the stock, port and vinegar to the boil and pour into the casserole. Cover and bake for 2½ hours or until the venison is tender.

Meanwhile, cut the lid off the pumpkin, then remove seeds and fibres. Carefully remove chunks of pumpkin flesh, but don't puncture the outer wall, and fill it with boiling water for a few minutes prior to serving up the dish. Put the pumpkin flesh into the casserole. Thicken the sauce with a roux if it seems too thin.

Pour the contents of the casserole into the pumpkin shell and serve on a large dish, garnished with elderflower fritters, buttered parsnips, halved tomatoes filled with rowan jelly and creamed potato cakes garnished with chopped chives. If you oil the outside of the pumpkin and place a garnish of red berries and leaves on the top, it looks particularly attractive. Your choice of berries will depend on the season.

ANGEL'S HAIR WITH PEACHES
Serves 6

3 small cantaloupe melons
3 medium-size fresh but firm peaches
4 oz (100 g) caster sugar
3 tablespoons fresh lime juice
6 teaspoons bottled rosewater
Finely shaved ice (optional)

Cut the melons in half. Discard the seeds and any stringy pulp, then finely shred the remaining flesh. Place in a deep container and pour any juice from the discarded melon shells over the 'angel's hair'. Wipe the peaches, split them in half and cut them into little cubes. Add the peaches, sugar, lime juice and rosewater to the melon.

Toss gently and refrigerate for about 3 hours, or until thoroughly chilled. Spoon into individual glasses. Brush the angel's hair with a few slivers of shaved ice.

REV. JOHN FERNLEY

Most armchair gourmets know something of the range of French provincial cooking, haute cuisine and perhaps even a variety of Indian regional dishes. Our weekly diet features dishes from all over the world as a matter of course, but we have lost sight of our culinary roots! Many traditional English dishes disappeared as convenience food began to appear on the shelves. With this in mind, and allied to my love of the providence of the wild, I have chosen to cook Mallard Pudding. It is very rich and filling, very easy to prepare, and absolutely delicious.

MALLARD PUDDING
Serves 6

1 wild duck
1 bay leaf
Fresh parsley and rosemary
8 oz (225 g) shin of beef
4 oz (100 g) ox kidney
8 oz (225 g) self-raising flour
4 oz (100 g) shredded suet
Salt and pepper
Mace

Choose a duck that has been hung for a couple of days and reserve the giblets, especially the liver. Remove all the meat from the duck (a bit messy this) and put the carcass in water to cover, with the bay leaf and herbs. Simmer to make a rich stock. Meanwhile, cut the beef and kidney into small pieces and cube the duck meat.

Make the suet pastry by mixing the flour, suet, a good pinch of salt and enough cold water to give a stiff dough. Roll it out and, using two-thirds of the pastry, line an old-fashioned pudding basin. Put in the meat, and season to taste with salt, pepper and mace. Add enough stock to cover the meat, and use the reserved pastry to form a lid.

Cover the basin with greaseproof paper and foil, then steam the pudding in an enormous pan of boiling water for 3 hours. The water should come halfway up the side of the pudding basin; add more water as necessary.

Serve the pudding with fresh, young carrots and turnips cooked whole, or with Brussels sprouts cooked with onion in chicken stock, and roasted potatoes.

A Crozes Hermitage would complement the rich-tasting pudding very well.

SYLLABUB
Serves 6

Honey
Lemon juice
White wine
1 pint (600 ml) double cream

Whisk together all the ingredients, until stiff, then put into 6 tall glasses, and chill before serving.

VICKI LAWSON-BROWN
I have chosen this meal because it is a firm family favourite. The ingredients need to be of good quality and very fresh; some of them are difficult to find in the North East but the hunt is well worth the effort, and other ingredients are brought back from holidays abroad. The meal is not difficult to cook and in the main can be prepared in advance.

CALVES' SWEETBREADS WITH PINEAU DES CHARENTES AND WILD MUSHROOMS
Serves 4 to 6

2 oz (50 g) carrots, diced
2 oz (50 g) onions, diced
2 oz (50 g) gammon, diced
1 tablespoon unsalted butter
1 bouquet garni
2 lb (1 kg) calves' sweetbreads, soaked and trimmed
5 fl oz (150 ml) Pineau des Charentes (a fortified wine)
10 fl oz (300 ml) good beef stock
1 handful of horn-of-plenty mushrooms
½ oz (15 g) cornflour
Salt and pepper

Pre-heat the oven to 325°F (160°C), gas mark 3.
Sauté the diced vegetables and gammon slowly in butter with

the bouquet garni until tender. Add the sweetbreads to the pan and cook for about 5 minutes. Transfer the sweetbreads to a heatproof casserole. Add the Pineau to the pan and reduce. Add the reduced liquid to the sweetbreads with the bouquet garni and enough stock to cover. Add the mushrooms, then cook in the oven for about 45 minutes. Allow to cool in the cooking stock until ready to serve.

Just before serving, remove the sweetbreads from the stock and slice thinly. Reduce the remaining liquid and discard the bouquet garni. Blend the cornflour with a tablespoon of Pineau and beat into the stock. Correct the seasoning and fold the sliced sweetbreads in. Serve with salsify and potatoes.

Salsify: peel and steam until just tender. Add a little lemon juice, seasoning and a little double cream before serving.

Potatoes: use a variety like French Cornichon. Boil in their skins until just tender, season, toss in unsalted butter and sprinkle with chopped parsley.

FRISÉE SALAD WITH PINE NUTS AND HAZELNUT DRESSING

Frisée lettuce
Pine nuts

For the dressing:
6 tablespoons hazelnut oil
1 tablespoon cassis vinegar
Salt and pepper
½ teaspoon tarragon mustard

Mix the dressing and pour over the frisée lettuce before serving. Sprinkle with pine nuts.

CHOCOLATE AND ARMAGNAC POTS
Serves 6

8 oz (225 g) plain chocolate (good quality)
4 egg yolks
10 fl oz (300 ml) single cream
3 tablespoons Armagnac
A little whipped cream
Slivered almonds

Melt the chocolate in the top part of a double saucepan or, more easily, in a microwave. Add the melted chocolate to the egg yolks, cream and Armagnac and liquidise for 30 seconds. Pour into glasses or ramekins and chill until set. Decorate with cream and slivered almonds before serving with langues de chat.

LANGUES DE CHAT

2 oz (50 g) butter
2 oz (50 g) caster sugar
2 egg whites
2 oz (50 g) plain flour (sieved)
Few drops vanilla essence
Butter for greasing

Pre-heat the oven to 400°F (200°C), gas mark 6. Cream the butter and sugar until fluffy. Whisk the egg whites lightly and gradually beat into the mixture with the flour and vanilla essence. Transfer to a piping bag with a nozzle, and pipe onto a greased baking sheet. Bake for 10 minutes. Transfer to a wire rack to cool.

MARGARET LOH

My grandmother was a fantastic cook and there were a lot of memorable Sunday lunches at my grandparents' house. These were my childhood's most favourite treat. My grandmother came from Indonesia, hence the strong Indonesian influence on the meal. We always had the following fish with chilled pickled cucumber, which was marinated with white vinegar, sugar and sesame oil. There are no words to describe the mango mousse, and I used to offer to lick the bowl for her. I have chosen the menu because it brings back happy childhood memories.

GRANDMOTHER'S FISH
Serves 6

1 small coconut or 5 oz (150 g) desiccated coconut
½ teaspoon garam masala
2 teaspoons cumin seeds
3 teaspoons coriander seeds
4 tablespoons vegetable oil
4 garlic cloves, crushed
6 thick halibut, cod or haddock steaks

2 tablespoons crunchy peanut butter
1 teaspoon soy sauce
Grated rind and juice of 2 limes
1-2 teaspoons chili powder (optional)
4 teaspoons brown sugar
Freshly ground black pepper and salt
1 large or 2 small avocados, peeled and sliced
1 large onion, thinly sliced, tossed in 2 tablespoons
seasoned cornflour
2 tablespoons chopped spring onion
2 oz (50 g) toasted desiccated coconut to garnish

Pre-heat oven to 375°F (190°C), gas mark 5.

Drain the juice of the coconut by using a skewer to pierce through the 3 holes at the top. Crack the coconut with the back of a strong chopper or a hammer. Use a sharp knife to cut out the white flesh, then finely shred about 5 oz (150 g) of flesh. Measure 5 fl oz (150 ml) juice and bring to the boil with the shredded coconut. If using desiccated coconut, bring to the boil in the same amount of water. Leave to cool.

Fry the spices in an oven-proof casserole dish with 2 tablespoons oil over a medium heat. Add the garlic and, when brown, add the fish steaks and brown both sides slightly, then remove from the heat. Mix 4 fl oz (120 ml) water, the peanut butter, soy sauce, lime juice and rind, chili powder, sugar, salt and pepper in a saucepan over a gentle heat, and then pour into the casserole. Bring to the boil, then bake for 15 to 20 minutes, covered.

Meanwhile, squeeze out the juice by pressing the coconut hard through a sieve, or use your hands. Put the coconut juice in the casserole and bring to the boil for a few minutes. Stir in the avocado slices and cover the pan. With the lid on, let the avocado slices heat through. Fry the cornflour-coated onion rings in oil. Garnish the casserole with fried onion rings, chopped spring onions and toasted coconut.

MANGO MOUSSE
Serves 6

2 large mangoes, peeled and chopped
1 tablespoon orange liqueur
1 pint (600 ml) whipping cream
Grated rind and juice of ¼ orange
2-3 tablespoons icing sugar
1 kiwi fruit, peeled and sliced
1 small orange, peeled and sliced

Purée the mangoes with the orange liqueur. Whip the cream with the orange rind, juice and sugar in a blender until slightly stiff. Fold in the mango purée. Pour into a large glass bowl. Decorate with alternate slices of kiwi and orange. Chill, then serve.

MARJORIE SMEDLEY

This rewarding meal is inexpensive and simple to prepare. It pleases friends, with its contrasts of bright colours and textures, and its slight air of adventure. Much of the preparation can be done the day before. And if a vegetarian friend comes, no problem – there's plenty of choice. Children, too, like the colours and enjoy scraping out the pudding dish.

ROAST OF BACON
Serves 6

3 lb (1.5 kg) hock of smoked bacon
4 big onions
2 tablespoons sunflower or similar oil
Salt
10 fl oz (300 ml) apple juice
1 teaspoon dry mustard
Coarsely ground black pepper
2 tablespoons marmalade or apple jelly

Pre-heat the oven to 350°F (180°C), gas mark 4.

Put the bacon into a roomy pan with water to cover and bring to the boil. Discard the water and dry the joint. Brush over with a little of the oil. Peel and slice the onions and fry briskly in the remaining oil for 1 minute. Season with salt. Put the onions in a baking dish not much larger than the bacon and place the bacon on top. Pour over the apple juice. Bake for 45 minutes.

Remove the bacon from the oven and put it on a carving board. Neatly slice the rind off and deeply score the fat in thin parallel strips, but not deeply enough to reach the meat. Sprinkle the dry mustard over the surface and rub it into the cracks. Blend or sieve the onions and adjust the seasoning. Put the bacon and onion back in the baking dish. Continue cooking for a further 45 minutes, adding more apple juice if the sauce dries up. The fat will be crisp and browned. Rub in ¼ teaspoon of black pepper, spread the marmalade or apple jelly over the surface and return to the oven for 5 to 10 minutes to caramelise. Keep an eye on it, as it burns quickly. Once cooked, the joint will keep in a low oven, covered, for some time. Serve the sauce separately.

RED CABBAGE
Serves 6

1 large red cabbage of good size
2 sliced onions
Dried peel of 2 tangerines
3 or more cooking apples, cut in chunks
1 cup of soft brown or demerara sugar
Salt
1 cup of wine vinegar or cider vinegar

Remove any discoloured cabbage leaves and trim the stem. Thinly slice the cabbage, stem and all. Put the onions in a large pan, followed by the cabbage, the tangerine peel torn into small pieces, and the apples. Add the sugar and salt, then the vinegar and 5 fl oz (150 ml) water, but do not stir. Cover and cook over a low heat for at least 1½ hours, then adjust the balance of sweet to sour and check the salt. You can add a few spoonfuls of chutney or jam, to improve the texture. Continue cooking, if needed, until the cabbage is neither too firm nor soft and pulpy. This accommodating dish will keep warm without harm, or if made the day before, it heats up perfectly.

STIR-FRY VEGETABLES
Serves 6

Carrots, parsnips, potatoes, swede, Jerusalem artichokes, if available
2-3 tablespoons sunflower or corn oil
1 sliced green pepper
2½ fl oz (65 ml) beef or vegetable stock
Salt
Juice of 1 lemon
1 tablespoon butter (optional)
A few chopped spring onions

Cut the root vegetables and artichokes as for thin chipped potatoes. Heat a large frying pan or wok over the highest heat and keep up the heat while cooking. Add the oil. Toss in all the vegetables except the spring onions, and keep them moving, so they don't stick. Cook, stirring, for 2 minutes. Add the stock. Remove from the heat. Season with salt and lemon juice and cover for a few minutes, to briefly steam the vegetables. (They must be crisp.) Add a little butter, if you wish, toss, scatter over the spring onions and serve at once.

WATERCRESS SALAD
Serves 6

2 bunches watercress, stems and all
4–6 oz (100–175 g) daikon, or mooli, sliced crossways
A handful of parsley

Tear the watercress into manageable pieces and mix with the daikon and parsley. Toss with a simple mild vinaigrette.

VINAIGRETTE
Use as good an oil as you can get, such as green Portuguese olive oil or a nut oil, and add three parts of oil to one of cider vinegar. Season sparingly with salt and ground pepper. Shake vigorously in a bottle or put in the blender.

DOWNUPSIE PUDDING WITH BITTER-LEMON SAUCE
Serves 6

For the sponge:
1 small carton plain yoghurt
½ carton sunflower or corn oil
2 eggs
2½ cups plain flour plus 1 teaspoon baking powder
2½ cups sugar (or 1 cup sugar and 2 tablespoons honey)

For the filling:
3 oz (75 g) butter or margarine
3 oz (75 g) soft brown sugar
1 teaspoon Angostura Bitters
Grated rind of 2 lemons
3 lb (1.5 kg) Conference pears, peeled and quartered
4 oz (100 g) shelled walnut halves
A few glacé cherries, halved

Pre-heat the oven to 350°F (180°C), gas mark 4.
Mix all the ingredients for the sponge and beat well for 1 to 2

minutes. Grease a flat-bottomed, 3-in (7.5-cm) high, oven-proof dish. Mix the butter and sugar and spread generously in the dish. Sprinkle a good few shots of Angostura Bitters over the bottom of the dish, with the grated lemon rind. Slice each pear quarter into 3 thin wedges and place in fan shapes over the bottom of the dish. Use the walnut halves and halved cherries, both flat side up, to make an attractive pattern. Chop the remaining pears and add to the sponge mixture. Pour into the dish and spread the mixture to cover the fruit. Bake for about 45 minutes. Check that it is cooked through and give it another 10 minutes if needed.

Slip a knife round the edges to free the pudding and turn it, complete with its bitter-lemon sauce, 'downupsie' onto a serving dish. Serve with *fromage frais* or cold single cream.

WILLIAM WATTERS

The starter looks scrumptious, and the combination of crispy pastry, succulent chicken, prawns and the tingly sauce is unbelievable. The main course, lamb cooked in minutes, holds all its flavour. The richness of the sauce balances well with spinach and the underlying garlic. I cook the vegetables in a microwave, again to retain flavour. For pudding, crunchy pastry boats containing apples al dente and fresh raspberries are a delicious sweet for children and adults alike.

CHICKEN AND PRAWNS IN A FILO ROSE
Serves 6

4 oz (100 g) butter
12 sheets filo pastry
4 chicken breasts
6 oz (175g) peeled prawns
4 fl oz (120 ml) white wine
Salt and white pepper
1 bay leaf
5 fl oz (150 ml) double cream

For the garnish:
Lettuce and radicchio leaves
Tomatoes
Broad-leaved parsley

Pre-heat the oven to 350°F (180°C), gas mark 4.

Melt the butter. Cut the filo sheets in thirds to make 3 long strips from each sheet. Then cut the strips in half to make 6 rectangles. Brush 6 tin-foil pie tins, 4 in (10 cm) in diameter, with melted butter, then in fours arrange the filo in layers inside the tins. Lay the second layer at right angles to the first. Carefully fan the leaves and continue with the third layer, brushing each leaf with butter as you go. Bake for 6 minutes or until gold and crisp, then leave to cool.

Meanwhile, wrap the chicken breasts and prawns in foil, adding a dot of butter, 2 tablespoons white wine, a pinch of salt and white pepper and a bay leaf. Seal and steam for 8 minutes, then strain the chicken and prawns, retaining the liquid. Keep the chicken and prawns warm. Melt the remaining butter, then strain the poaching liquid into it. Add the rest of the wine and reduce by half. Whisk in the double cream. Slice the chicken breast across the grain into ½-in (1-cm) slices. Combine with the prawns.

Blanch and peel the tomatoes, then deseed them. Cut the tomato flesh into smallish triangles. Decorate a plate with ribbons of lettuce and radicchio. Place a filo rose on each plate. Fill each filo rose with chicken and prawns. Pour the sauce on top. Dot with tomato pieces and chopped parsley, and serve.

LAMB FILLET ON SPINACH
Serves 6

2 lb (1 kg) lamb cut from the leg in ½-in (1-cm) slices
6 tablespoons butter
10 fl oz (300 ml) red wine, preferably Merlot
2 onions, thinly sliced
1 garlic clove
2 lb (1 kg) fresh spinach
Salt and pepper
10 fl oz (300 ml) home-made beef stock
6 tablespoons redcurrant jelly
Mint to garnish
6 tomato roses

Cut any sinew or fat from the lamb, to get 'rounds' of meat. Slice each steak horizontally part-way through, then open it up, like a butterfly. Smack it with a cleaver, but not too flat. Fry the lamb in butter over medium heat, removing when droplets of blood begin to emerge on top. Keep the lamb warm between 2 plates. Deglaze the pan juices with a glass of wine.

In a large saucepan cook half the onions in butter, then add the crushed and chopped garlic. Add the washed spinach. Season with salt and pepper, and cook until tender, then drain, chop finely and keep warm. Cook the remaining onions in the lamb pan, then add the stock and wine with the pan juices and reduce to make a thickish sauce. Strain and keep warm.

Pour about 3 tablespoons of sauce onto each plate, then make an island of spinach and arrange the lamb on top. Put 1 tablespoon of redcurrant jelly in the middle. Garnish with a mint leaf and top with a tomato rose. Serve with baby carrots, broccoli florets and creamed potatoes.

PASTRY BOATS
Serves 6

6 oz (175 g) plain flour
4 oz (100 g) caster sugar
2 oz (50 g) unsalted butter, chopped
1 egg
1 lb (450 g) fresh or frozen raspberries
4 dessert apples
2 tablespoons butter
10 fl oz (300 ml) double cream

Pre-heat the oven to 375°F (190°C), gas mark 5.

To make the pâte brisée pastry, mix the flour and 2 oz (50 g) sugar together. Place on a clean worktop, and make a well in the centre. Put the chopped butter and egg into the well and work into the dry ingredients with your fingertips, until the dough forms a ball. Place in a polythene bag and leave in the refrigerator for 30 minutes. Roll out to a thickness of ¼–¹⁄₁₆ in (5 mm–1.5 mm). This part is very tricky. Using a broad palate knife to lift the pastry, line 6 little boat-shaped baking tins with it, and prick the bases with a fork to allow any air to escape while baking. Bake for 6 minutes, keeping an eye on them. Remove and leave to cool.

Put 1 tablespoon caster sugar and the raspberries in a blender and reduce to a liquid, then rub through a sieve to remove seeds. Peel and slice the apples. Melt a little butter in a pan. Add the apples with the remaining caster sugar. Cook until the apples take on a brown edge and the sugar has caramelised. Pour raspberry sauce onto each plate, then put a spoonful of cream in the middle. Fill the pastry boats with the apples and their juice. Place the boats on top of the cream, then pull the cream out with a cocktail stick to make a ship's wake. Whip the remainder of the cream, and add a spoonful to each boat to make a 'puff of smoke'.

INDEX

Entries in italics refer to wine or to the titles of publications.

L

M

N

O

P